Table of Contents

Introduction

To ACT or not to ACT? That really is the question! Often one of the first questions a student asks themselves is, "Should I take the SAT, the ACT, or both tests?" You've likely also wondered, "Since I did well on the SAT already, do I really need to study for the ACT?" or, "Should I even bother taking it at all???" These are very important questions. Since the policy for receiving test scores varies among institutions, one of the first steps to answering your questions is to contact the admission offices of the schools you are interested in attending to learn about their policy. Next, you should become aware of the important differences between the two tests. Many students will assume that the two exams are interchangeable – this isn't so! If you want to gain the highest notice and available options as possible, you should consider taking both tests.

- The ACT is an achievement test, designed to assess what you have learned in school. The SAT is an aptitude test which uses math and verbal knowledge as means by which to test your reasoning abilities, rather than what you have learned.

- The ACT has a science test which covers various topics in physics, chemistry, biology, and earth sciences. The ACT also has a writing test, which is optional. However, in the SAT, the writing test is required – and science testing is a separate exam altogether (SAT Subject Tests).

- The SAT consists of 140 questions, plus an essay, and is given for three hours and forty-five minutes. The ACT consists of 214 questions and an optional essay, and is given for three hours and twenty-five minutes, which decreases the average time allowed for each question.

- The ACT math test covers in-depth geometry as well as basic trigonometry. Only basic geometry is found on the SAT.

- The ACT does not have a wrong answer penalty; you should never leave a question blank. The SAT, however, has a ¼ point per wrong answer penalty; you only want to guess if you have reduced your answer choices.

- The questions on the ACT tend to stay within the same range of difficultly, whereas the SAT has questions which vary in difficulty.

- Scoring differs considerably. The total maximum score for the ACT is 36. There is a maximum of score of 800 for *each* of the three SAT test sections – 800 for math, 800 for writing, and 800 for critical reading (total maximum score of 2400).

- The SAT allows the student to first view their scores, and then decide which scores they wish to have sent to their chosen schools. With the ACT, you only have until the Thursday after the Saturday you took the test to make any changes or cancellations – you don't get to view the scores first.

The ACT – A Detailed Overview

Now that you have a better understanding of the two tests in a side-by-side comparison, you need to know the details of the ACT and how it works. The ACT is a multiple choice test which covers four general areas; mathematics, science, English, and reading. There is also an optional writing test in which an essay is written from a given prompt. The main test takes about three and a half hours to complete (including breaks). The test will take an additional thirty minutes, if you opt to take the writing test (which is recommended). The following is a breakdown of the exam:

- Science – 40 questions – 35 minutes
- Reading – 40 questions – 35 minutes
- Mathematics – 60 questions – 60 minutes
- English – 75 questions – 45 minutes
- Writing – 1 prompt – 30 minutes

Scoring on the ACT

The number of questions answered correctly on the four individual sections composes the raw scores. These are then converted into a scaled score, after taking into account the differences between test versions; the score ranges from 1 (lowest) to 36. A composite score is then calculated by averaging the four scaled scores, with the highest score being 36. The math, English and reading sections are also given sub-scores ranging from 1 – 18.

The essay written for the writing section is graded by two individuals on a scale of 1 – 6. These scores are then totaled, resulting in a writing sub-score that ranges from 2 (lowest) to 12. This score is then combined with the English test scores to give the English/writing score; the English test counts as 2/3 of the combined score.

Chapter 1: Let's Make a Plan

No great venture starts without a plan. Your score depends on you making a solid study plan. Opening up practice questions and just jumping in won't help. You need to find your strengths and weaknesses, so that you know where to focus your time. Doing practice tests will come later.

Your Study Plan

Schedule your Study Time: Schedule when you will study each day and stick to it. If you have a specific amount of time set aside to work on preparing yourself, you won't have the added stress of wondering if you are doing enough.

Schedule your Breaks: This is just as important as scheduling your study time. You will stay motivated and focused if you know that you get to go for a walk, or read something else, or watch a little TV in the near future. Give yourself 10-15 minutes of break time for every hour that you study.

Short Term Goals: Set achievable goals each day (or week) for the material you want to cover. This will help you stay focused on a subject or topic. There is a lot to study, and you need to be sure that you are proceeding systematically, so that you don't waste time repeatedly covering the same material.

Actively Read: Don't let yourself skim through subjects. You might as well turn your brain off and stare at the wall, because you will get nothing out of your time. As you read, actively think about what you have read and anticipate what you will read next. If you find yourself passively reading, take your study break and refocus.

Write Things Down: This means using pen and paper. The act of physically transferring ink to paper will help you solidify in your mind what you are studying. Trust us on this. It will take a little more time while you study, but you won't waste time later going back through the same material over and over.

Study Locations: Find a quiet, relaxing place that you can dedicate as a "study zone." Library: good. In front of TV: bad. This location should NOT be your bed, or the couch, or anywhere else you use for sleeping, eating, or relaxing. If you sit at your desk at home, or in the library, you won't be tempted to "watch TV for just a few minutes," or start nodding off because you are in already bed.

Sleep: No surprise here! You need sleep. To prepare yourself, and to help control your nerves when test day comes, get in the habit now of following the same routine each night and going to bed at the same time. Lying awake staring at the ceiling the entire night before the test won't do much good for your score.

Practice Tests: "How many should I take?" Our recommendation is no more than two. However, you should never take a practice test before you've studied just to "see how well you can do." We suggest that you first focus on the individual math, reading, writing, science, and English concepts as outlined in this book. Once you are up to speed on a concept, go through the practice questions at the end of that section. When you are doing well on the practice problems, *then* you may move on to a full practice test. Remember, practice tests don't help you get better on the individual concepts. They give you an indication of what your score range will be and help you practice focusing for a full 3 hours and 25 minutes. Practice tests also give you a feel for the timing of the test sections, so you can learn to pace yourself. If you don't perform as well as you'd like on the first practice test, review and practice the concepts you missed before attempting another full practice test. If you need additional help, check out the "Resources and Help" section of this book.

Test Day

The Night Before: Take the evening off from studying. Give your mind and body a chance to relax. Eat a healthy dinner with good carbohydrates and get a good night's rest.

Food: On the day of the test, avoid excess coffee and caffeine. Eat a breakfast with lots of fruits, grains, and lean protein to boost your energy and keep you full. Don't substitute sugary candies or sodas for energy.

Think Positively: Seriously! Imagine yourself seeing the questions and thinking confidently, "Hey, I know this answer!"

Be Bold: Don't second-guess questions. Go with your gut instinct, but don't be careless. Make your decision and move forward. Worrying about a question from two pages ago won't help you answer the question you are on now.

Don't Panic: You are prepared. You worked diligently during study time and practice tests and know your own pace. Don't rush, and don't worry about the clock or what anyone else is doing.

Gum: Students who chew gum during a test score higher on average than those who don't. Chewing gum keeps you awake and focused. Find your favorite flavor and don't leave home without it on test day. Double-check beforehand that your test-taking center allows gum.

Cramming: Do NOT do this! It will only stress you out. And really…come on…do you think you'll actually accomplish something in a couple hours that you couldn't in the weeks you spent studying beforehand?

What to Bring: You MUST have: your admission ticket, two No. 2 pencils with a soft eraser, your photo ID, and an acceptable calculator (graphing or scientific is best, not four-function). As these tests are designed so that anyone can take them, even without a calculator, a simple calculator is all that you really need.

You may **NOT** use a calculator with the following functions:

- Calculators with built-in computer algebra systems
- Texas Instruments: TI – 89, TI – 92
- Hewlett-Packard: hp 48GII, and all models beginning with hp 40G, hp 49G, or hp50G
- Casio: Algebra fx 2.0, ClassPad 300, and all models beginning with CFX-9970G
- Pocket organizers
- Handheld or laptop computers
- Electronic writing pads or pen-input devices
- Calculators with a typewriter keypad (QWERTY)
- Calculators built into cell phones or other electronic devices

You SHOULD bring: A watch with which you are familiar and have used during your practice tests, extra batteries for your calculator, a bag or backpack for your belongings, and drinks and snacks for breaks.

What to Leave at Home: Scratch paper, notes and books, cell phones, MP3 players/iPods, highlighters and colored pencils, a timer (like a kitchen timer), or any type of photographic equipment or listening/recording device.

Applying to College

College Admission Standards: Research each university's average, or standard, for acceptance. Remember to factor in your grades, extracurricular activities, etc. This will eliminate fear of the unknown and give you a target ACT score to work toward.

Talk with Counselors: Counselors at your high school may know of some great resources for you, as well as help you decide what your goals should be for college. Also, talk with admission advisors at the colleges you're interested in. You'll find that there is a lot that they don't tell you in the brochure! Give yourself every advantage possible.

Be Yourself: When you write essays for college applications, don't try to write what you think "they" want to read. Admission boards receive thousands of empty, generic, and meaningless essays every year, which they promptly disregard. Be yourself and write to your unique strengths. Your ACT score is just a number, but that number gives colleges a reason to look at you; when they do, take advantage of it and be yourself.

Chapter 2: Study Tricks, Tips, and Cautions

As mentioned earlier, the ACT focuses on testing your knowledge of concepts; it is not a reasoning exam. However, you will still need to exercise caution to avoid distracters. Distracters are answer choices which seem too easy or are otherwise designed to trick you into choosing them. If you aren't on your game and ready for them, you'll waste time or – worse yet – answer incorrectly because you were not prepared to ignore the distracters. Stay focused on applying your knowledge, but keep an eye out for distracters as well.

Everyone has strengths and weaknesses, and you need to identify yours. Be honest; maybe you just aren't as good at math as you would like to be. This is your opportunity to improve. If you are only getting 75% of the math portion's potential score, even if you are getting 95% of the reading and writing correct, then there are still a lot more points you could be making on math. Don't think that a strong reading or writing score will make up for a weaker math score…start working on getting better at math and pick up those extra points.

Next, we've all been there…answering "C" ten times in a row. Is this a trick? That must be wrong! Did you mess something up? The answer is simple: no. It's not a trick, and you didn't do anything wrong. If this happens, don't let it distract you!

You will probably come across questions to which you don't know the answer. On the ACT, you do not lose points for wrong answers, so NEVER leave an answer choice blank! If you can, narrow your choices down. The more answers you can eliminate, the greater chance you have of guessing the correct answer. For example: if you can eliminate all but two answer choices, then you have already increased your odds of guessing corrects to 50%. If you can't narrow the answer choices down to two, leave it blank, move on, and come back later if time permits. If you get down to the last couple of minutes and still have many unanswered questions, always go through and bubble them in.

Develop a system for marking off the answers in the question book that you know are wrong. Do not cross off answers on the answer sheet – you don't want to risk any stray marks getting left behind. Whatever system you adopt, be consistent. You don't want to have to think, "Wait. Did that circle mean it's good, or did that check mark mean it's good?"

When should you really dig in and start studying? Base your schedule on when you will be taking the test, instead of studying first and then seeing what test dates are available. Visit collegeboard.org to see the available dates in your area, preferably at a location you are familiar with. Then, work backwards to figure out how many weeks or months you have prior to the test, and make a schedule accordingly. Be sure to leave a few extra weeks open, just in case you need a little more time.

Chapter 3: The Science Reasoning Section

Overview

The Science Reasoning section of the ACT consists of seven groups of information (presented in passages, charts, tables, graphs, etc.), which cover multiple areas of science, such as astronomy, biology, chemistry, physics, earth, and life sciences. You will have 35 minutes to answer a total of 40questions. Although you are not expected to have taken courses in all the subject areas covered, the ACT does expect you to be able to use your reading comprehension and reasoning skills, as they apply, to the information you are given. Some questions require you to understand contextual knowledge, expressions, basic facts, and theories about the information. Each passage is followed by several multiple-choice questions. Success is determined by your ability to quickly comprehend the information presented to you.

The information will be presented in three different formats:

- **Research Summaries:** Detailed narrative of one experiment or several correlated experiments.
- **Conflicting Viewpoints:** Multiple, differing theories about a scientific question.
- **The Data Representation:** Scientific information is presented in tables, graphs, or figures that summarize specific research.

Basic Skills Necessary

The science test requires you to: critically evaluate data and scientific arguments, recognize relationships, make generalizations, and draw conclusions. Be prepared to make simple mathematical calculations using the data. Some questions require you to understand background knowledge, terms, basic facts, and concepts about the information.

As with all the ACT test sections, know the directions ahead of time.

Directions for the Science Reasoning Section:
Each of the seven passages in this test is followed by several questions. After you read each passage, select the correct choice for each of the questions that follow the passage. Refer to the passage as often as necessary to answer the questions. You may NOT use a calculator on this test.

General Tips

1. Refer to the passage for each question. Do not attempt to answer using your background knowledge or your memory of the passage. Answers are based on the data and information presented in the information given, not on what you did in a class.

2. You will have to work quickly. If you break it down, you have approximately five minutes to read each passage and answer the associated questions. Try to take only two or three minutes to study each passage. This will leave about twenty to thirty seconds for each of the questions.

3. Highlight the main points and other items which you feel are pertinent as you read.

4. During practice exams, try quickly skimming over the questions (but not the choices) before reading the passage, as well as the traditional read-and-answer, to see which works best for you. You may find that this approach is not only faster, but increases your percentage of correct answers by allowing you to focus on the key words in the questions.

5. Make sure you're answering the right question and referring to the right data set, hypothesis, or study.

Tips for Individual Formats

The following are tips for each of the different formats, along with the percentage of questions found on the test.

Research Summaries (45%)

1. The majority of the questions presented in the research summaries format require you to comprehend the purpose of the experiment.

2. Pay close attention to the experimental or study design, the methods used, and the results.

3. Be watchful for information or hypotheses which are not directly stated in the data that **may or may not** be drawn from the experiment.

4. Be able to recognize conclusions that can be drawn from the design of the study or experiment, as well as from the results.

5. Know how the data was obtained, retained, and displayed.

Conflicting viewpoints (17%)

1. Start by rereading the opening sentence of the passage to make sure that you know the scientific issues in dispute.

2. Recognize the main points of disagreement in the theories presented, since many of the *questions are based on these*. Try not to let the details of the given information interfere with recognizing the main points.

3. Focus on the key differences in the viewpoints, such as possible weaknesses in an argument and information that might strengthen or support a viewpoint.

4. Pay attention to additional information given in a question.

5. Keep in mind conflicts and contradictions; underlying assumptions in the viewpoints; as well as possible biases, and valid criticisms, of a viewpoint.

Data Representation (38%)

1. Focus on understanding what information is given.

2. Don't go by memory. Always refer to the visual representation (graph, chart, etc.) for each question.

3. Peruse the presented data carefully, looking for high and low points, as well as fluctuations and trends.

4. Review headings, factors, and/or descriptive facts given, noting the differences and correlations.

5. Pay attention to how the data is presented, such as how the terms are used in each representation (total, control, dependent, independent, etc.).

Test Your Knowledge – Science Reasoning

Asteroid-Impact Theory

The dinosaurs disappeared at the end of the Mesozoic era, about 65 million years ago. The disappearance took place over a very short period of time and was, according to some scientists, triggered by Earth colliding with a large asteroid.

Today, evidence of this collision can be found in the rock record. Geologists have discovered a thin layer of clay containing a high concentration of the element iridium between two particular rock layers. This boundary marks the end of the Mesozoic and the beginning of the Cenozoic era. This iridium-rich layer has been identified at the Mesozoic-Cenozoic boundary at many different locations around the world. Iridium, while rare on Earth, is a common substance in meteorites and asteroids.

The asteroid not only supplied the iridium, but its white-hot rock fragments also started fires that engulfed entire continents. The soot from these fires, combined with asteroid and crustal particles that were propelled into the atmosphere, blocked out the Sun's energy. The lack of sunlight halted photosynthesis and caused a decrease in global temperatures. Much of the plant and animal life, including the dinosaurs, could not adapt to the temperature change and died.

Gradual-Extinction Theory

Some scientists disagree with the asteroid-impact theory. They point to evidence which suggests that the dinosaurs died out gradually because of a long-term climatic change. Earth experienced increased volcanic activity 65 million years ago. This volcanism could have produced the iridium, but, more importantly, those volcanoes did produce tremendous amounts of carbon dioxide. The increased levels of carbon dioxide in the atmosphere prevented Earth from radiating excess heat back into space, and thus caused a worldwide warming.

The warming of Earth is what caused the dinosaurs' disappearance. After examining dinosaur egg fossils, paleontologists discovered that the eggshells became thinner in at least one species. This was thought to be the result of heat adversely affecting the dinosaurs' metabolism. These thin-shelled eggs, which were easily broken, lowered the survival rate among the offspring and contributed to the eventual extinction of the dinosaurs.

1. Astronomers recently estimated that only 3% of asteroids, with orbits that intersect Earth's, have been identified. This finding adds support to the asteroid impact theory by:

A) Increasing the likelihood of past Earth-asteroid collisions.
B) Showing how little astronomers know about asteroids.
C) Proving that iridium-rich asteroids are common in the solar system.
D) Showing that many asteroids are too small to be easily identified.

2. A geologist examines a sedimentary rock layer from the Mesozoic-Cenozoic boundary. According to the asteroid-impact theory, the geologist should not expect to find:
   A) A high concentration of iridium.
   B) A high concentration of soot particles.
   C) Evidence of great volcanic activity.
   D) Fossilized plant remains.

3. What do supporters of the asteroid-impact theory assume about the fires started by the white-hot asteroid fragments?
   A) They spread quickly and were wide-ranging.
   B) They removed carbon dioxide from the atmosphere, causing a global cooling.
   C) They burned the vegetation, limiting the food supply.
   D) They produced high levels of carbon dioxide, causing a global warming.

4. Both theories presented in the passage cite which of the following factors as contributing directly to the dinosaurs' extinction?
   A) High levels of soot and volcanic ash.
   B) High concentrations of iridium.
   C) Global temperature change.
   D) Increased amounts of carbon dioxide introduced into the atmosphere.

5. Mass extinctions throughout history often occur in conjunction with drops in the sea level. What would proponents of the gradual-extinction theory have to demonstrate in order to tie those facts together?
   A) Mass extinctions and drops in the sea level are both caused by increased volcanic activity.
   B) The greenhouse effect causes lowering of the sea level as well as gradual mass extinctions.
   C) With less water available, fires run rampant and destroy the food supply.
   D) Drops in the sea level and mass extinctions are caused by the same changes in climate.

6. After examining the 250-million-year fossil record, two paleontologists have uncovered evidence suggesting that the rate of species extinctions peaks every 26 million years. Supporters of the asteroid-impact theory would most likely favor which of the following explanations for this finding?
   A) Some massive object periodically disrupts the solar system, causing comets and asteroids to enter the inner solar system.
   B) The tilt of Earth's axis changes every 26 million years, causing long-term climatic changes which lead to mass-extinction episodes.
   C) Earth's orbit becomes more elliptical every 26 million years; and it travels farther from the Sun, which causes periods of global cooling.
   D) Earth's global weather patterns change in response to the size of the polar ice caps, plunging Earth into a global cooling pattern every26 million years.

Test Your Knowledge Answers – Science Reasoning

1. **A)** (Analyzing)
2. **C)** (Understanding)
3. **A)** (Understanding)
4. **C)** (Analyzing)
5. **D)** (Generalizing)
6. **A)** (Generalizing)

Chapter 4: The Reading Section

The ACT reading section consists of 40 questions, with a 35 minute time limit. The reading test has four somewhat-lengthy passages on the subjects of humanities, social studies, natural sciences, and prose fiction. The reading section is fairly cut and dry. Simply read the passage and answer the questions. The challenge is the amount of reading you need to do, quickly and comprehensively.

You will receive three scores:

- One overall
- A sub-score for social studies and natural sciences
- A sub-score humanities and prose fiction

All passages in each section have numbers along the left side of the text which indicate the line number. There are ten questions for each passage covering the following:

1. Specific details and facts
2. Comparisons and analogies
3. Inferences
4. Word meaning through context
5. Main idea of sections or the passage as a whole
6. Character identification and motivation
7. Cause and effect
8. Author's tone and/or point of view

The Humanities passage topics are culturally based, focusing on the arts and literature, and can be written journalistically, analytically, or as a personal essay. These tend to portray varying degrees of bias, which you will need to take into account when reading.

The Social Studies passage topics are focused on the workings of civilizations and societies and usually have a political perspective. Take notice of dates, names, chronological order, key concepts, and cause and effect relationships. The authors tend to express controversial views about the subject. It is important that you are able to separate the author's point of view from the general argument.

The Natural Science passages present experiments and scientific theories, along with their implications and reasoning. These are going to include considerable facts and data. Pay attention to comparisons, as well as cause and effect.

The Prose fiction passages are usually excerpts from short stories or novels. You'll want to take note of the plot, characters, style, and tone.

TEST SECRET

Make notes! Underline or mark important details as you read to speed up finding the information if you need to return to the passage.

As with all the ACT test sections, know the directions ahead of time.

Directions for the Reading Section:
On this test you will have 35 minutes to read four passages and answer 40 questions (ten on each passage). Each set of ten questions appears directly after the relevant passage. You should select the answer choice that best answers the question. There is no time limit for work on the individual passages, so you can move freely between passages and refer to each as often as you'd like.

The following "Test Your Knowledge" section will give you an opportunity to practice reading a passage and answering questions – just as you will on the ACT. While a good vocabulary can help, the only way to get better at the reading section is to practice, practice, practice. It is, however, vitally important that you practice the way you want to perform on test day. Form good habits now by actively reading and making notes.

Test Your Knowledge – Reading Section

The following is an excerpt from Henry David Thoreau's essay "Civil Disobedience," written in 1848.

I HEARTILY ACCEPT the motto,—"That government is best which governs least";[1] and I should like to see it acted up to more rapidly and systematically. Carried out, it finally amounts to this, which also I believe,—"That government is best which governs not at all"; and when men are prepared for it, that will be the kind of government which they will have. Government is at best but an expedient; but most governments are usually, and all governments are sometimes, inexpedient. The objections which have been brought against a standing army, and they are many and weighty, and deserve to prevail, may also at last be brought against a standing government. The standing army is only an arm of the standing government. The government itself, which is only the mode which the people have chosen to execute their will, is equally liable to be abused and perverted before the people can act through it. Witness the present Mexican war,[2] the work of comparatively a few individuals using the standing government as their tool; for, in the outset, the people would not have consented to this measure.

This American government—what is it but a tradition, though a recent one, endeavoring to transmit itself unimpaired to posterity, but each instant losing some of its integrity? It has not the vitality and force of a single living man; for a single man can bend it to his will. It is a sort of wooden gun to the people themselves. But it is not the less necessary for this; for the people must have some complicated machinery or other, and hear its din, to satisfy that idea of government which they have. Governments show thus how successfully men can be imposed on, even impose on themselves, for their own advantage. It is excellent, we must all allow. Yet this government never of itself furthered any enterprise, but by the alacrity with which it got out of its way. It does not keep the country free. It does not settle the West. It does not educate. The character inherent in the American people has done all that has been accomplished; and it would have done somewhat more, if the government had not sometimes got in its way. For government is an expedient by which men would fain succeed in letting one another alone; and, as has been said, when it is most expedient, the governed are most let alone by it. Trade and commerce, if they were not made of India rubber,[3] would never manage to bounce over the obstacles which legislators are continually putting in their way; and, if one were to judge these men wholly by the effects of their actions, and not partly by their intentions, they would deserve to be classed and punished with those mischievous persons who put obstructions on the railroads.

But, to speak practically and as a citizen, unlike those who call themselves no-government men,[4] I ask for, not at once no government, but at once a better government. Let every man make known what kind of government would command his respect, and that will be one step toward obtaining it.

After all, the practical reason why, when the power is once in the hands of the people, a majority are permitted, and for a long period continue, to rule, is not because they are most likely to be in the right, nor because this seems fairest to the minority, but because they are physically the strongest. But a government in which the majority rule in all cases cannot be based on justice, even as far as men understand it. Can there not be a government in which majorities do not virtually decide right and wrong, but conscience?—in which majorities decide only those questions to which the rule of expediency is applicable? Must the citizen ever for a moment, or in the least degree, resign his conscience to the legislator? Why has every man a conscience, then? I think that we should be men first, and subjects afterward. It is not desirable to cultivate a respect for the law, so much as for the right. The only obligation which I have a right to assume is to do at any time what I think right. It is truly enough said that a corporation has no conscience; but a corporation of conscientious men is a corporation with a conscience. Law never made men a whit more just; and, by means of their respect for it, even the well-disposed are daily made the agents of injustice. A common and natural result of an undue respect for law is, that you may see a file of soldiers, colonel, captain, corporal, privates, powder-monkeys,[5] and all, marching in admirable order over hill and dale to the wars, against their wills, ay, against their common sense and consciences, which makes it very steep marching indeed, and produces a palpitation of the heart. They have no doubt that it is a damnable business in which they are concerned; they are all peaceably inclined. Now, what are they? Men at all? Or small movable forts and magazines, at the service of some unscrupulous man in power?

[1] Possible reference to "The best government is that which governs least," motto of the *United States Magazine and Democratic Review* (1837–1859), or "The less government we have, the better," from Ralph Waldo Emerson's "Politics" (1844), sometimes mistakenly attributed to Thomas Jefferson.

[2] U.S.-Mexican War (1846–1848), considered by abolitionists to be an effort to extend slavery into former Mexican territory.

[3] Made from the latex of tropical plants. "India," because it came from the West Indies, and "rubber," from its early use as an eraser.

[4] Anarchists, many of whom came from Massachusetts

[5] Boys who carry gunpowder for soldiers.

1. This essay could best be characterized as:
- A) A diatribe against the government.
- B) An abolitionist speech.
- C) A citizen's call to action.
- D) An anarchist's desire for change.
- E) A conservative's words of praise.

2. The dominant rhetorical device in line 3 is:
- A) Oxymoron.
- B) Parallel structure.
- C) Paradox.
- D) Inverted syntax.
- E) Catalogue.

3. The author draws a connection between the "standing government" and the "standing army" to argue that the army and the government:

- I. Are only aspects of a whole.
- II. Can be distorted and mistreated.
- III. Are manipulated by a minority.

- A) I only
- B) II only
- C) III only
- D) II and III only
- E) I, II, and III

4. Footnote 2 serves to do all of the following *except*:
- A) Justify America's participation in the Mexican-American War.
- B) Explain why the author and others did not support the war.
- C) Provide insight into the abolitionist cause.
- D) Supply the dates of the Mexican-American War.
- E) Suggest a possible outcome of the Mexican-American conflict.

5. The "American government" is juxtaposed to "a single living man" to argue that the government is all of the following *except*:
- A) Moribund.
- B) Easily manipulated.
- C) Ineffectual.
- D) Without real power.
- E) Without energy.

6. The author's point about "the people" and their expectations of government is that the government must be:
   A) Convoluted yet quiet.
   B) Mechanistic yet calm.
   C) Robotic and disturbing.
   D) Intricate and noisy.
   E) Complex and alarming.

7. "Yet this government…out of its way", in lines 21 – 22, means that:
   A) The government helps itself by helping the people's business ventures.
   B) The government helps people progress, through its support and effort.
   C) Quickly removing itself from the path of the people is the only help the government can offer.
   D) Forcefully inserting itself into the activities of its people helps them to succeed.
   E) A slow and well-thought-out governmental response leads to the success of the people.

8. Lines 22 – 23 use which rhetorical device and for what purpose?
   A) Polysyndeton to reveal the qualities of the American people.
   B) Asyndeton to underscore why the American people should be proud.
   C) Allusion to refer to America's recent historical past.
   D) Abstract diction to create ambiguity about American achievements.
   E) Anaphora to emphasize what the government has not done.

9. The author's point regarding conscience is best stated as:
   A) Conscience should be subservient to the law.
   B) To be a subject entails abiding by the precepts of one's conscience.
   C) Individual conscience is more important than the law.
   D) Men have consciences, as reflected in the morality of legislators.
   E) It is the duty of conscience to obey the laws of legislators.

10. The author's tone in the passage as a whole is best described as:
   A) Warmly sympathetic.
   B) Harshly critical.
   C) Unquestioningly supportive.
   D) Staunchly judgmental.
   E) Insightfully creative.

Test Your Knowledge Answers – Reading Section

1. A) This is an overview question in which you must consider the essay as a whole. A diatribe is a bitter, verbal attack on somebody or something. In this case, the attack is aimed at the government and those who follow it unquestioningly. However, let's say you don't know the word "diatribe." The other answers can be eliminated, thus leaving you with A as the best choice. There is nothing in the speech about the abolishment of slavery. The only reference to slavery occurs at the essay's end, and this reference is more about the government than it is about abolishing slavery; thus, B can be eliminated. A call to action entails inspiring people to create change. The essay's topic is not governmental change, but governmental problems. The speaker is not an anarchist and, in fact, differentiates himself from this group in lines 32–33, so answer D is incorrect. The author is not a conservative – he does not want to maintain the status quo. Thus, E is incorrect.

2. C) A paradox is a seemingly contradictory statement pointing to a truth. The author states "government is best which governs not at all" (line 3). A government that "governs not at all" is not a government. However, the author's larger point is that a government should govern, but only when matters of expedience are involved. He latter claims the government "is only the mode which the people have chosen to execute their will" (lines 9–10). As a mode, it is really the people who are governing themselves. If you know your rhetorical device definitions, then you can quickly eliminate A, D, and E. An oxymoron is a two-word contradiction like *terrible joy*. Inverted syntax is when the first words are in reverse order, such as "go then I will" for "I will go." Finally, a catalogue is another word for a list. None of these devices appear. Parallel structure may seem to be an attractive distracter because these lines contain some interesting syntactical arrangements; however, parallel structure (or parallelism) occurs when similar grammatical or syntactical patterns are repeated. Example: I enjoy swimming in a pool, fishing in a pond, and discussing literature in a classroom. Again, parallelism does not occur in the lines cited.

3. D) Reasoning can be found in lines 6 – 10. He first mentions the army, then states that, "the government [...] is equally liable to be abused and perverted [...]" "Equally liable" is the clue to choosing II, as "equal" implies both the army and the government. Of course, you would also have to understand the meanings of "perverted" and "abused." Choice II contains synonyms for these words. Choice III is justified by lines 11 and 12: "Witness the present Mexican war, the work of *comparatively a few individuals* using the standing government as their tool." As the government controls the army, it stands to reason that the army, too, is manipulated by a few. Choice I is attractive. In lines 8 and 9, the author states, "The standing army is only an arm of the standing government." However, only the army is an aspect of the whole. No such claim is made about the government.

4. A) Questions about footnotes have become part of the multiple-choice section, so you should expect to see them. In providing dates and explaining the probable effects of the war, answers D and E are a given. The implications of this information are expressed in answers B and C.

5. C) The author claims the government lacks the "vitality and force" of the individual. Thus A and E are correct because "energy" is a synonym for vitality and "moribund" means nearly dead. Nearly dead implies a loss of vitality. Answer B is also correct as the remaining sentence states "for a single man can bend it to his will," indicating manipulation. Answer D is correct because force and power are connotatively the same.

6. D) Another word for "complicated" is intricate, and "din" is noise (line 18). Knowledge of vocabulary again comes in handy. C and E are attractive distracters, but are incorrect because in answer E "alarming" is incorrect and in answer C "disturbing" is incorrect. If you know the meaning of "din," you can easily eliminate A and B.

7. C) Again, vocabulary knowledge is useful. "Alacrity" means speedy readiness; it implies swiftness. The author's point in these lines is that the only help the government can offer its citizens is to be ready to move swiftly out of the way should an individual want to engage in a venture that involves risk.

8. E) Anaphora is the repetition of phrases at the beginning of sentences. The author repeats "It does not…" three times in three successive sentences. Repetition emphasizes or underscores. E is the answer because the author is emphasizing what the government has not done. "It" is the pronoun for the antecedent "government."

9. C) If you got question 3 correct, you should be able to choose the correct answer here. The key points regarding this answer are: "We should be men first and subjects afterward…" (line 44), and "The only obligation which I have a right to assume is to do at any time what I think right" (lines 45 – 46). The juxtaposition of "men" to "subject" reveals that, for the author, to be a man entails following one's own conscience, regardless of what those in power demand. "Subject" here is used in the sense of someone who is under the rule of a higher authority. If you understand these key points, the other answers can be eliminated quite quickly. Answers A, B, and E are the reverse of what the author claims; D is incorrect because though the author does make the point that men have consciences, he does not claim the same is true for legislators.

10. B) Throughout the essay, the author has been critical of the government itself, governmental legislators, men who align themselves with the government, and men who follow the laws of the government unthinkingly. Think back to how the author describes the men in the army and the men who "serve the state." Pretty harsh and critical, right? The most attractive distracter is answer D. However, D is incorrect because judgment does not connote the same disapproval as criticism entails. Further, the author is condescending and disparaging in his comments, rather than firm and steadfast (the meaning of staunch). Certainly the author is firm in his opinions, but again, the criticisms are harsh rather than firm. Answer A and C can be easily eliminated because they are the opposite of the author's comments. E can be eliminated because the author does not offer a creative solution to what he discusses; he merely condemns.

Chapter 5: The Math Section

The math section of the ACT test consists of 60 questions, in which you have 60 minutes to complete them. This section consists of three sub-scores, each based on the following subject areas:

- **Pre-Algebra and Elementary Algebra (40%)**: square roots, exponents, algebraic expressions, absolute value, linear equations, probabilities.

- **Intermediate Algebra and Coordinate Geometry (30%)**: quadratic formula, rational and radical expressions, statistics, functions, complex numbers, inequalities, graphing, distance, midpoint, equations of lines, slope, simultaneous equations, binomials and polynomials.

- **Plane Geometry and Trigonometry (30%)**: properties of plane figures, volume, transformations, 3-D geometry, trigonomic properties, trigonomic functions and graphing, using trigonomic identities to solve equations.

Remember, there is no wrong answer penalty, so do not leave an answer selection blank. However, since the objective is to get as many right as possible, eliminate as many choices as possible before choosing.

Since you only have a minute to answer each question, go through and answer all of the questions that are easy to you first, then go back and tackle the others.

The Most Common Mistakes

Here is a list of the six most common mistakes test takers make on the ACT, starting with the most common:

- Answer with the wrong sign (positive / negative)
- Working questions in order
- Order of Operation errors when solving
- Misplaced decimal
- Solution does not respond to what was asked for in the question
- Circling the wrong letter or filling in wrong circle

If you're thinking, "Those ideas are just common sense" – exactly! Most of the mistakes made on the ACT are simple mistakes. Regardless, they still result in a wrong answer and the loss of a potential point.

Strategies

1. Go back to the basics – first and foremost, practice your basic skills, such as sign changes, order of operations, simplifying fractions, and equation manipulation. These are the skills you will use the most on the ACT; they will

just be applied in different contexts. Remember that when it comes right down to it, there are still only four basics used to solve any math problem: adding, subtracting, multiplying, and dividing. The only thing that changes is the order with which they are used to solve the problem.

2. Don't rely on mental math – using mental math is great for eliminating answer choices, but ALWAYS WRITE IT DOWN! This cannot be stressed enough. Use your paper and booklet; by writing and/or drawing out the problem, you are more likely to catch the common mistakes. Just the act of writing something down for every question leads to an improvement in your ACT score, by forcing you to organize your calculations. Use your calculator to *check* your work.

3. The Three Times Rule:

1) **Read the question** – Write the given information.

2) **Read the question** – Set up equation(s) and solve.

3) **Read the question** – Make sure your answer makes sense (is the amount too large or small, is the answer in the correct unit of measure, etc.).

4. Making an educated guess – Eliminate the answer choices you are relatively sure are incorrect, and then guess the most likely correct from the remaining choices. Educated guessing is critical to increasing your score.

Calculators

Calculators may only be used on the mathematics section, but all the questions can be answered without one. You may use any four-function, scientific, or graphing calculator, unless it has the following features which are prohibited.

As stated before, you may **NOT** use a calculator with the following functions:

- Calculators with built-in computer algebra systems
- Texas Instruments: TI – 89, TI – 92
- Hewlett-Packard: hp 48GII, and all models beginning with hp 40G, hp 49G, or hp50G
- Casio: Algebra fx 2.0, ClassPad 300, and all models beginning with CFX-9970G
- Pocket organizers
- Handheld or laptop computers
- Electronic writing pads or pen-input devices
- Calculators with a typewriter keypad (QWERTY)
- Calculators built into cell phones or other electronic devices

You may bring a backup calculator and batteries. The testing facility staff will check your calculator to ensure that it meets the requirements. The testing facility staff will also monitor your usage throughout the test to ensure that you are complying with the rules of use.

Math Concepts Tested on the ACT

Before you take the ACT, you want to make sure that you have a good understanding of the math topics covered; you will also want to sharpen your basic skills. This section will explain what math areas are covered on the exam with brief, but detailed, examples; however it is NOT designed to TEACH you the math.

The next few pages will cover various math subjects (starting with the basics, but in no particular order), along with worked examples. If you are taking the ACT, you have already had course instruction in these areas. Keep in mind that this is a guide to what you can expect to encounter on the Math ACT and is not a comprehensive lesson to teach you everything which you have been taught previously in school.

You need to practice in order to score well on the test. To make the most out of your practice, use this guide to determine the areas in which you need more review, and practice all areas under testing circumstances. Do not time yourself on the first practice test. You should take your time and let your brain recall the necessary math. The examples given will 'jog' your memory. Then, when you feel you are ready, begin taking timed tests. This is another important part of scoring well on the ACT: knowing your strong areas and the average amount of time it takes to solve the problems. It also helps relieve stress while taking the test.

Practice exams can help you to become familiar with the types of questions there are on the test, how many there are, and what to expect.

TEST SECRET

DO NOT go through countless practice exams as a means to become "better" at math. Going through all those exams will take too much time, burn you out, and it won't help!

If you find yourself needing additional help with math concepts after reviewing the following information, refer to the "Math Resources" chapter at the end of this book.

- Order of Operations

  PEMDAS – **P**arentheses/**E**xponents/**M**ultiply/**D**ivide/**A**dd/**S**ubtract

- Positive & Negative Number Rules

  (+) + (-) = subtract the two numbers. Solution gets the sign of the larger number

  (-) + (-) = negative number

  (-) * (-) = positive number

  (-) / (-) = positive number

  (-) / (+) = negative number

  (-)*(+) = negative number

- Absolute Value

  The absolute value of a number is its distance from zero, not its value.

  Example:
  $|3| = 3$ and $|-3| = 3$

- Arithmetic Sequence

  Each term is equal to the previous term plus *x*.

  Example: 2, 5, 8, 11 x = 3
  3 + 2 = 5, 3 + 5 = 8, 3 + 8 = 11…

- Geometric Sequence

  Each term is equal to the previous term multiplied by *x*.

  Example: 2, 4, 8, 16 $x = 2$
  2 * 2 = 4, 2 * 4 = 8, 2 * 8 = 16…

- Prime Factorization

  Expand to prime number factors.

  Example: 104 = 2*2*2*13

  Multiply common prime factors

  Example: 28 = 2*2*7
  80 = 2*2*2*5

- Greatest Common Factor (GCF)

  The greatest factor that divides two numbers.

  Example: the GCF of 24 and 18 is 6. 6 is the largest number, or greatest factor, that can divide both 24 and 18.

- Percent, Part, & Whole

  Part = Percent * Whole

  Percent = Part / Whole

  Whole = Part / Percent

  Example: Jim spent 30% of his paycheck at the fair. He spent $15 for a hat, $30 for a shirt, and spent $20 playing games. How much was his check? (Round to nearest dollar)
  ANSWER: Whole = 65 / .30 = $217.00

  TEST SECRET

  Remember, you must put the % into decimal form before solving!

  For more help on Percent, Part, & Whole, see Section 1 of the Math Question Bank.

- Percent Change
  - Percent change = amount of change / original amount * 100
  - Percent increase =
    (new amount – original amount) / original amount * 100
  - Percent decrease =
    (original amount – new amount) / original amount * 100
  - Amount increase (decrease) =
    original price * percent markup (markdown)
  - Original price = new price / (whole - percent markdown)
  - Original price = new price / (whole + percent markup)

  Example: A car that was originally priced at $8300 has been reduced to $6995. What percent has it been reduced?

  (8300 – 6995) / 8300 * 100 = 15.72%
  ANSWER: 15.72%

For more help on Percent Change, see Section 1 of the Math Question Bank.

- Repeated Percent Change

Increase: Final amount = original amount * $(1 + \text{rate})^{\text{\# of changes}}$
Decrease: Final Amount = original amount * $(1 - \text{rate})^{\text{\#of changes}}$

Example: The weight of a tube of toothpaste decreases by 3% each time it is used. If it weighed 76.5 grams new, what is its weight in grams after 15 uses?

Final amount = $76.5 * (1 - .3)^{15}$
ANSWER = $76.5*(.97)^{15}$ = 48.44 grams

TEST SECRET

This formula is used to calculate annual bank interest problems with number of years being the exponent.

For more help on Repeated Percent Change, see Section 1 of the Math Question Bank.

- Simple Interest

Interest * Principle

Example: If I deposit $500 in an account with an annual rate of 5%, how much will I have after 2 years?

1st yr 500 + (500*.05) = 525
2nd yr 525 + (525*.05) = 551.25
ANSWER: $551.25

For more help on Simple Interest, see Section 1 of the Math Question Bank.

- Ratios

To solve a ratio simply find the equivalent fraction. To distribute a whole across a ratio:

1. Total all parts.
2. Divide the whole by the total number of parts.
3. Multiply quotient by corresponding part of ratio.

Example: There are 90 voters in a room, who are either Democrat or Republican. The ratio of Democrats to Republicans is 5:4. How many Republicans are there?

Step 1 $5 + 4 = 9$

Step 2 $90 / 9 = 10$

Step 3 $10*4 = 40$

ANSWER: 40 Republicans

For more help on Ratios, see Section 10 of the Math Question Bank.

- Proportions

Direct Proportions: Corresponding ratio parts change in the same direction (increase/decrease).

Indirect Proportions: Corresponding ratio parts change in opposite directions; as one part increases the other decreases.

Example: A train traveling 120 miles takes 3 hours to get to its destination. How long will it take if the train travels 180 miles?

120mph: 180mph is to *x* hours: 3 hours
(write as fraction and cross multiply)

$120/3 = 180/x$

$540 = 120x$

$x = 4.5$ hours

For more help on Proportions, see Section 10 of the Math Question Bank.

- Mean

Mean is a math term for "average." Total of all terms / number of terms.

Example: What is the average of 2, 10, 17, and 30?

$(2+10+17+30)/4 = 14.75$

ANSWER: 14.75

The following is an example of a mean problem with missing information.

Example: Cory averaged 3 hits per game over the course of 5 baseball games. He had 2 hits in the first and fourth games, 3 hits in the second game, and 4 hits in his last game. How many hits did he have in his second game?

Step 1:
Determine total. 3 hits*5 games = 15 hits

Step 2:
Determine known total. 2 +2 + 3 + 4 = 11

Step 3:
Subtract. 15 – 11 = 4

ANSWER: 4 hits in his second game

- Median

The median is the middle number of a given set. In the case of a set of even numbers, the middle two numbers are averaged (mean).

Example: What is the average of 1, 2, 3, 4, 5, 6, & 7?
ANSWER: 4

Example: What is the median of 1, 2, 3, 4, 5, 6, 7, & 8?
ANSWER: 4.5

- Mode

The mode is the number that occurs most frequently within a given set.

Example: what is the mode of 1, 2, 4, 3, 2, 5, 6, 7, 7, 2?
ANSWER: 2

For more help on Mean, Median, & Mode, see Section 2 of the Math Question Bank.

- Combined Average

Working a combined average problem is similar to finding a simple average, except you must weight each average before determining the sum.

Example: If Cory averaged 3 hits per game during the summer and 2 hits per game during the fall and played 7 games in the summer and 8 games in the fall, what was his hit average overall?

Step 1:
Weigh each average.

Summer: 3 * 7 = 21
Fall: 2 * 8 = 16
Sum = 37

Step 2:
Total number of games. 7 + 8 = 15

Step 3:
Calculate average. 37/15 = ~2.47 hits/game

ANSWER: Approximately 2.47 hits per game

How to work a combined average problem with a missing term:

Example: Bobbie paid an average of $20 a piece for ten shirts. If five of the shirts averaged $15 each, what was the average cost of the remaining shirts?

Step 1:
Calculate sum. 10 * 20 = 200

Step 2:
Calculate sub-sum #1. 5 * 15 = 75

Step 3:
Calculate sub-sum #2. 200 – 75 = 125

Step 4:
Calculate average. 125 / 5 = 25

ANSWER: $25

For more help on Combined Averages, see Section 2 of the Math Question Bank.

- Exponent Rules
  - $x^0 = 1$ Example: $5^0 = 1$
  - $x^1 = x$ Example: $5^1 = 5$
  - $x^a \cdot x^b = x^{a+b}$ Example: $5^2 \times 5^3 = 5^5$
  - $(xy)^a = x^a y^a$ Example: $(5*6)^2 = 5^2*6^2 = 25*36$
  - $(x^a)^b = x^{ab}$ Example: $(5^2)^3 = 5^6$
  - $(x/y)^a = x^a/y^a$ Example: $(10/5)^2 = 10^2/5^2 = 100/25$
  - $x^a/y^b = x^{a-b}$ Example: $5^4/5^3 = 5^1 = 5$ (remember $x \neq 0$)
  - $x^{1/a} = \sqrt[a]{x}$ Example: $25^{1/2} = \sqrt[2]{25} = 5$
  - $x^{-a} = \frac{1}{x^a}$ Example: $5^{-2} = \frac{1}{5^2} = \frac{1}{25}$ (remember $x \neq 0$)
  - $(-x)^a$ = positive number if a is even; negative number if a is odd

TEST SECRET

It is crucial that you know how to simplify and solve exponents and roots on the ACT. Practice these as much as needed until you master them!

Example:

Simplify the following: $\frac{(3^{-1}a^4 b^{-3})^{-2}}{(6a^2ab^{-1}c^{-2})^2}$

$$\frac{(3^{-1}a^4 b^{-3})^{-2}}{(6a^2ab^{-1}c^{-2})} = \frac{3^2a^{-8}b^6}{6^2a^4b^{-2}c^{-4}}$$

$$= \frac{9a^{-8}b^6}{36a^4b^{-2}c^{-4}} = \frac{b^6b^2c^4}{4a^4a^8} = \frac{b^8c^4}{4a^{12}}$$

ANSWER: $= \frac{b^8c^4}{4a^{12}}$

To add or subtract equations with exponential terms, calculate the term value, then add or subtract.

Example:
$18^0 - 3 + 2^4 = 1 - 3 + 16 = 14$
ANSWER: 14

For more help on Exponents, see Section 3 of the Math Question Bank.

- Roots

Root of a Product: $\sqrt[n]{a \cdot b} = \sqrt[n]{a} \cdot \sqrt[n]{b}$

Root of a Quotient: $\sqrt[n]{\frac{a}{b}} = \frac{\sqrt[n]{a}}{\sqrt[n]{b}}$

Fractional Exponent: $\sqrt[n]{a^m} = a^{m/n}$

Example: Simplify the following:

$$\frac{2(6-3\sqrt{5})}{(6+3\sqrt{5})(6-3\sqrt{5})}$$

$$= \frac{12-6\sqrt{5}}{6^2-(3\sqrt{5})^2}$$

$$= \frac{12-6\sqrt{5}}{6^2-(3\sqrt{5})^2} = \frac{12-6\sqrt{5}}{6^2-(3\times 3\times\sqrt{5}\times\sqrt{5})}$$

$$= \frac{12-6\sqrt{5}}{6^2-(9\times 5)} = \frac{12-6\sqrt{5}}{36-45} = \frac{12-6\sqrt{5}}{-9} = -\frac{(12-6\sqrt{5})}{9}$$

$$= -\frac{3(4-2\sqrt{5})}{9} = -\frac{(4-2\sqrt{5})}{3} = \frac{-4+2\sqrt{5}}{3}$$

$$= \frac{-4+2\sqrt{5}}{3}$$

ANSWER: $= \frac{-4+2\sqrt{5}}{3}$

For more help on Roots, see Section 3 of the Math Question Bank.

- Algebraic Equations

When simplifying or solving algebraic equations, you need to be able to utilize all math rules: exponents, roots, negatives, order of operations, etc.

1. Add & Subtract: only the coefficients of like terms.

Example:

$5xy + 7y + 2yz + 11xy - 5yz = 16xy + 7y - 3yz$

2. Multiplication: first the coefficients, then the variables.

Example: monomial*monomial

$(3x^4y^2z)(2y^4z^5) = 6x^4y^6z^6$

(a variable with no exponent has exponent of 1)

Example: monomial*polynomial

$(2y^2)(y^3+2xy^2z + 4z) = 2y^5 + 4xy^4z + 8y^2z$

Example: binomial*binomial

(remember **FOIL** – **F**irst, **O**uter, **I**nner, **L**ast)

$(5x + 2)(3x + 3)$

First	$5x \cdot 3x = 15x^2$
Outer	$5x \cdot 3 = 15x$
Inner	$2 \cdot 3x = 6x$
Last	$2 \cdot 3 = 6$
Combine like terms.	$15x^2 + 21x + 6$

Example: binomial*polynomial

$(x + 3)(2x^2 - 5x - 2)$

First term	$x(2x^2 - 5x - 2) = 2x^3 - 5x^2 - 2x$
Second term	$3(2x^2 - 5x - 2) = 6x^2 - 15x - 6$
Add	$2x^3 + x^2 - 17x - 6$

3. Division: same as multiplying. Be sure to follow exponent and root rules!

4. Difference of squares: remember **FOIL** – **F**irst, **O**uter, **I**nner, **L**ast

Examples:

$a^2 - b^2 = (a + b)(a - b)$

$a^2 + 2ab + b^2 = (a + b)(a + b)$

$a^2 - 2ab + b^2 = (a - b)(a - b)$

TEST SECRET

It is crucial that you know how to simplify and solve algebraic equations containing multiple exponents, variables, and roots. The ACT will have problems that contain multiple equations all in one problem, so practice these specific skills!

For more help on Algebraic Equations, see Section 4 of the Math Question Bank.

- Inequalities

Inequalities are solved like linear and algebraic equations, except the sign must be reversed when working with a negative.

Example: Solve: $-7x + 2 < 6 - 5x$

Step 1:
Combine like terms. $-2x < 4$

Step 2:
Solve for x. Reverse sign. $x > -2$

ANSWER: $x > -2$

Solving compound inequalities will give you two answers.

Example: Solve: $-4 \leq 2x - 2 \leq 6$

Step 1:
Add 2 to each term to isolate x. $-2 \leq 2x \leq 8$

Step 2:
Divide by 2. $-1 \leq x \leq 4$

ANSWER: Solution set is [-1, 4]

For more help on Inequalities, see Section 5 of the Math Question Bank.

- Literal Equations

These are equations with more than one variable. Solve in terms of one variable first.

Example: Solve for y: 6x = 9y = 1/3y + 3x

Step 1:

Combine like terms.

$$9y - 1/3y = 3x - 6x$$
$$26/3y = -3x$$

Step 2:

Solve for y.

$$y = -9x/26$$

ANSWER: y = -9x/26

For more help on Literal Equations, see Section 5 of the Math Question Bank.

- Linear Systems

A linear system requires the solving of two literal equations simultaneously. There are two different methods (Substitution and Addition) that can be used to solve linear systems on the SAT.

<u>Substitution Method</u>: Solve for one variable in one equation and substitute it into the other equation.

Example: Solve $3y - 4 + x = 0$ and $5x + 6y = 11$

Step 1: Solve for one variable.

$$3y - 4 + x = 0$$
$$3y + x = 4$$
$$x = 4 - 3y$$

Step 2: Substitute into second equation, and solve.

$$5(4 - 3y) + 6y = 11$$
$$20 - 15y + 6y = 11$$
$$20 - 9y = 11$$
$$-9y = -9$$
$$y = 1$$

Step 3: Substitute into first equation.

$$3(1) - 4 + x = 0$$
$$-1 + x = 0$$
$$x = 1$$

ANSWER: solution is x = 1, y = 1

Addition Method: Manipulate one of the equations so that when added to the other, one variable is eliminated.

Example: Solve $2x + 4y = 8$ and $4x + 2y = 10$

Step 1:

Manipulate one equation to eliminate a variable when added together.

$$-2(2x + 4y = 8) =$$
$$-4x - 8y = -16$$
$$+ 4x + 2y = 10$$
$$-6y = -6$$
$$y = 1$$

Step 2:

Plug into an equation and solve for the other variable.

$$2x + 4(1) = 8$$
$$2x + 4 = 8$$
$$2x = 4$$
$$x = 2$$

ANSWER: solution is $x = 2$, $y = 1$

Example: The following is a typical ACT word problem that would use a linear system to solve:

Tommy has a collection of coins worth $5.20. He has 8 more nickels than quarters. How many of each does he have?

Step 1:

Set up equations.

Let n = nickels and q = quarters. $\quad .05n + .25q = 5.2$

Drop the 0. $\quad n = q + 8$

Step 2:

Substitute equation 2 into equation 1. $\quad .05(q+8) + .25q = 5.2$

Step 3:

Solve for q. You can ignore the decimal point and negative sign after this step because you are solving for number of coins.

$$-.05(q+8) + .25q = 5.2$$
$$.05q+.4+.25q = 5.2$$
$$q = 16$$

Step 4:
Plug into other equation. $n = q + 8$ $n = 24$

Solution: 16 quarters, 24 nickels

Step 5:
Check your answer. 24(.05) + 16(.25) = \$5.20
\$1.20 + \$4.00 = \$5.20

ANSWER: 16 quarters, 24 nickels

EST SECRET

You must be able to solve a three-equation linear system: x, y, and z. The problems are solved the same way, except after the first step you have 2 variables left, so you must repeat the process one more time.

There are three types of linear systems:

- **Consistent: There is one solution. (see our worked example above)**
- **Inconsistent: There is no solution, so the answer doesn't fit when checked.**
- **Dependent: There are infinite solutions.**

Finally, remember to check your work and especially pay attention to your signs!

For more help on Linear Systems, see Section 5 of the Math Question Bank.

- Rate of Change

Used to describe the change in one variable with respect to another. The average rate of change of y with respect to x is: change in y / change in x.

Example: The percentage of the U.S. population living in rural areas decreased from 84.7% in 1850 to 21.0% in 2000. What was the average rate of change in the rural population annually over that time period?

Step 1:
Set up the equation putting the dependent variable in the numerator.

change in % /change in years
(21.0 – 84.7)/ (2000-1850) =
-63.7% / 150 years
~ - 0.42 years

Since the problem stated a decrease, a negative answer is correct. The population decreased on average .42% each year.

ANSWER: .42% each year

TEST SECRET

Remember, if this is a grid-in answer, omit the leading zeros and it must be a decimal, not a percentage. In this example, only grid in .0042, and not 0.0042.

For more help on Rate of Change, see Section 10 of the Math Question Bank.

- Slope (m)

The same formula is used to calculate the slope (m) of a straight line connecting two points.

$m = (y_2 - y_1) / (x_2 - x_1)$ = change in y / change in x

Example: Calculate slope of the line in the diagram.

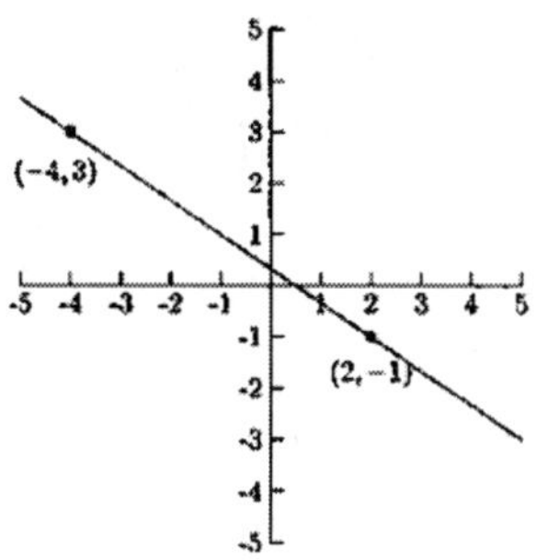

m = (3 – (-1))/(-4 – 2) = 4/-6 = - 2/3

ANSWER: -2/3

TEST SECRET

Remember, when calculating slope, it isn't important which point you designate (x1,y1) as long as you are consistent throughout your problem.

For more help on Slope, see Section 6 of the Math Question Bank.

- Distance and Midpoint

To determine the distance between two points from a grid use the formula:

$$d = \sqrt{(x_2 - x_1)^2 + (y_2 - y_1)^2}$$

Example: What is the distance between point (3, -6) and (-5, 2)?

$d = \sqrt{(-5-3)^2 + (2-(-6))^2} = \sqrt{64+64} = \sqrt{64 \ x \ 2} = 8\sqrt{2}$

To determine the midpoint between two points:

- Add the two x coordinates together and divide by 2 (midpoint x).
- Add the y coordinates together & divide by 2 (midpoint y).

$$= \left(\frac{x_1 + x_2}{2}, \frac{x_1 + x_2}{2}\right)$$

For more help on Distance and Midpoints, see Section 6 of the Math Question Bank.

- General Linear Equations

Know how to find your x, y coordinates and slope using this equation:
y = b + mx

For more help on Linear Equations, see Section 6 of the Math Question Bank.

- Absolute Value Equations

Remember you will have two answers.
$|x| = a$ x = -a and x = a

Each equation must be solved separately and all solutions must be checked into the original equation.

Example: Solve for x: |2x – 3| = x + 1

2x – 3 = - (x +1) and 2x – 3 = x + 1
2x – 3 = -x – 1
3x = 2

ANSWER: x = 2/3 and x = 4

For more help on Absolute Value Equations, see Section 7 of the Math Question Bank.

- Quadratics

Factoring: converting $ax^2 + bx + c$ to factored form. Find two numbers that are factors of c and whose sum is b.

Example: Factor $2x^2 + 12x + 18 = 0$

Step 1:
If possible, factor out a common monomial. $2(x^2 - 6x + 9)$

Step 2:
Find two numbers that are factors of 9 and = -6 when added

2(x _)(x _)
-3, -3

Step 3:
Fill in the binomials. Be sure to check your answer and signs. $2(x – 3)(x – 3)$

Step 4:
To solve, set each to = 0.

$x – 3 = 0$ so $x = 3$

If the equation cannot be factored (there are no two factors of *c* that sum to = *b*), the quadratic formula is used.

$$x = \frac{-b \pm \sqrt{b^2 - 4ac}}{2a}$$

Use the same equation from the above example – a = 2, b = 12, & c = 18. Plug into the formula and solve. Remember, there will still be two answers due to the (+) and (-) before the radical.

You must solve for each. The following is an example of an ACT word problem that would use a quadratic equation to solve:

The square of a number is 8 less than 6 times the number. What numbers make this statement true?

Step 1:

Set up the equation. $x^2 = 6x – 8$

Step 2:

Put in standard form. $x^2 – 6x + 8 = 0$

Step 3:
Solve using either method.

$(x – 1)(x – 8)$
$x – 1 = 0$ $x = 1$
$x – 8 = 0$ $x = 8$

ANSWER: x = 1, x = 8

If the quadratic is a difference of two squares (b = 0 and c = n^2 for some number n), factor it into the product of a sum and a difference.

$x^2 - n^2 = (x - n)(x + n)$

TEST SECRET

If *c* is positive and *b* is positive, then the factors will both be positive. If *c* is positive and *b* is negative, then the factors will both be negative. If *c* is negative, the factors will have opposite signs.

For more help on Quadratics, see Section 7 of the Math Question Bank.

- Functions

Functions are simple, if you think of them as just another substitution problem. They are basically worked the same as any other equation. Pay attention to your math, always double check your signs, and check your answer.

The following is an example of a typical function problem, followed by function rules and definitions you need to know.

If $f(x) = x^2 + 3x$, find $f(x + 2)$.

Step 1:
Simply replace $(x + 2)$ for x. $x^2 + 3x$
$(x + 2)^2 + 3(x + 2)$

Step 2:
Use FOIL for first term. $x^2 + 4x + 4 + 3x + 6$

Step 3:
Combine like terms. $x^2 + 7x + 10$

Step 4:
Factor. $(x + 5)(x + 2)$

Step 5:
Set equations to zero. Solve. $x + 5 = 0$ so $x = -5$
$x + 2 = 0$ so $x = -2$

ANSWER: Solution set: - 2, - 5

Rules of Functions:

1. Adding: $(f + g)(x) = f(x) + g(x)$

   Example: If $f(x) = 3x + 2$ and $g(x) = x^2$, then $(f + g)(x) = 3x + 2 + x^2$

2. Subtracting: $(f - g)(x) = f(x) - g(x)$

   Example: If $f(x) = 3x + 2$ and $g(x) = x^2$, then $(f - g)(x) = 3x + 2 - x^2$

3. Multiplying: $(f \cdot g)(x) = f(x) \cdot g(x)$

   Example: If $f(x) = 3x + 2$ and $g(x) = x^2$, then $(f \cdot g)(x) = (3x + 2) \cdot x^2$

4. Dividing: $(f / g)(x) = f(x) / g(x)$, provided $g(x) \neq 0$

   Example: If $f(x) = 3x + 2$ and $g(x) = x^2$, then $(f / g)(x) = (3x + 2) / x^2$

5. Composition: $(f \circ g)(x) = f(g(x))$

   Replace each x in the formula of $f(x)$ with the entire formula of $g(x)$.

   Example: If $f(x) = x^2 - x$ and $g(x) = x - 4$,

   $(f \circ g)(x) = f(g(x))$ $\quad$ $(g \circ f)(x) = g(f(x))$

   $= f(x - 4)$ $\quad$ $= g(x^2 - x)$

   $= (x - 4)^2 - (x - 4)$ $\quad$ $= (x^2 - x) - 4$

   (can be reduced further)

6. Inverse: $f^{-1}(x)$ = the inverse of $f(x)$; denoted by $f(f^{-1}(x)) = f^{-1}(f(x)) = x$

   If two functions f(x) and g(x) are defined so that:

   $(f \circ g)(x) = x$ and $(g \circ f)(x) = x$

   then f(x) and g(x) are inverse functions of each other.

   To find the correct inverse function of f(x) every time, you can use this procedure:

   Given the function f(x) we want to find the inverse function, f -1(x).

   1. First, replace f(x) with y. This is done to make the rest of the process easier.
   2. Replace every x with a y and replace every y with an x.
   3. Solve the equation from Step 2 for y. This is the step where mistakes are most often made so be careful with this step.
   4. Replace y with f -1(x). In other words, we've managed to find the inverse at this point.

Example: If $f(x) = \frac{x-1}{x+1}$, find $f^{-1}(x)$

Step 1: $y = \frac{x-1}{x+1}$

Step 2: $x = \frac{y-1}{y+1}$

Step 3:

$$xy + x = y - 1$$
$$xy - y = -x - 1$$
$$y(x - 1) = -(x + 1)$$
$$y = \frac{-(x+1)}{(x-1)}$$

Step 4: $f^{-1}(x) = \frac{-(x+1)}{(x-1)}$

TEST SECRET

The ACT doesn't use the typical function symbol *f(x)*; instead you will see any variety of symbols between the variables like *xΩy* or *x·y* . To solve, just plug the given value into the places where their respective variables occur in the original equation:
Ex: If xΩy = 4 – *x/y, what is the value of 6Ω2:*
4 – (6/2) ANSWER=1

For more help on Functions, see Section 7 of the Math Question Bank.

- Dividing Equations

A polynomial by a monomial:

$$3x^3 + 6x^2 + 3x \div 3x = 3x^3/3x + 6x^2/3x + 3x/3x$$
$$= x^2 + 2x + 1$$

A polynomial by a polynomial:

$$\begin{array}{r} x^3 - 3x^2 + 6x - 4 \\ 2x - 3 \overline{\smash{\big)}\, 2x^4 - 9x^3 + 21x^2 - 26x + 12} \\ \underline{-(2x^4 - 3x^3)} \\ -6x^3 + 21x^2 - 26x + 12 \\ \underline{-(-6x^3 + 9x^2)} \\ 12x^2 - 26x + 12 \\ \underline{-(12x^2 - 18x)} \\ -8x + 12 \\ \underline{-(-8 + 12)} \\ 0 \end{array}$$

For more help on Dividing Equations, see Section 7 of the Math Question Bank.

- Graphing

You must be familiar with all the various aspects of graphing functions and quadratics, especially the following concepts:

1. Vertex: The turning point: Can be the minimum or the maximum. Has the coordinates (h, k). The vertex form of the quadratic equation is:

   $f(x) = a(x - h)^2 + k$ the vertex is at (h, k)

   The formula $(\frac{-b}{2a}, f(\frac{-b}{2a}))$ (correspond with the quadratic equation) can be used to find the vertex.

2. Axis of Symmetry: The line that runs through the vertex: the formula used is the same as finding for h above: $h = \frac{-b}{2a}$

3. Roots, Zeros, and Solutions: All the values of x which make the equation equal to zero, also known as x-intercepts.

4. Translations: The graph of $y = f(x - h) + k$ is the translation of the graph.

   $y = f(x)$ by (h, k) units in the plane.

   Translations follow these rules:
   $f(x) + k$ is $f(x)$ shifted upward k units
   $f(x) - k$ is $f(x)$ shifted downward k units
   $f(x + h)$ is $f(x)$ shifted left h units
   $f(x - h)$ is $f(x)$ shifted right h units
   $-f(x)$ is $f(x)$ flipped upside down ("reflected about the x-axis")
   $f(-x)$ is the mirror of $f(x)$ ("reflected about the y-axis")

5. Domain: All the possible x values of a function.

6. Range: All the possible output values ($f(x)$ or y values) of the function.

   For more help on Graphing, see Section 6 of the Math Question Bank.

- Geometry

The ACT math section requires a solid knowledge of geometry. No formulas are given. Below is a list of common terminology, facts, formulas, and fundamental principles with worked examples on those that tend to be a bit confusing.

Acute angle:	Measures less than 90°
Acute triangle:	Each angle measures less than 90°
Obtuse angle:	Measures greater than 90°
Obtuse triangle:	One angle measures greater than 90°
Adjacent angles:	Share a side and a vertex
Complementary angles:	Adjacent angles that sum to 90°
Supplementary angles:	Adjacent angles that sum to 180°
Vertical angles:	Angles that are opposite of each other: they are always congruent (equal in measure).
Equilateral triangle:	All angles are equal
Isosceles triangle:	Two sides and two angles are equal
Scalene:	No equal angles
Parallel lines:	Lines that will never intersect. Y ll X means line Y is parallel to line X
Perpendicular lines:	Lines that intersect or cross to form 90° angles
Transversal line:	A line that crosses parallel lines
Bisector:	Any line that cuts a line segment, angle, or polygon exactly in half
Polygon:	Any enclosed plane shape with three or more connecting sides (ex. a triangle)
Regular polygon:	Has all equal sides and equal angles (ex. square)
Arc:	A portion of a circle's edge
Chord:	A line segment that connects two different points on a circle
Tangent:	Something that touches a circle at only one point without crossing through it
Sum of Angles:	The sum of angles of a polygon can be calculated using $(n-1)180^{\circ}$ n = the number of sides

Know the names of sided plane figures:

Number of Sides and Name

3	triangle or trigon	11	hendecagon
4	quadrilateral or tetragon	12	dodecagon
5	pentagon	13	tridecagon
6	hexagon	14	tetradecagon
7	heptagon	15	pentadecagon
8	octagon	16	hexadecagon
9	nonagon	17	heptadecagon
10	decagon	18	octadecagon

Regular Polygons:

Polygon Angle Principle: S = sum of interior angles of a polygon with n-sides.

$$S = (n - 2)180$$

The measure of each central angle (c) is $360^\circ/n$
The measure of each interior angle (i) is $(n-2)180^\circ/n$
The measure of each exterior angle (e) is $360^\circ/n$

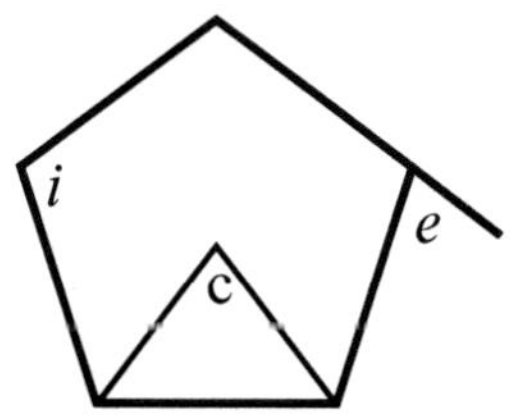

To compare areas of similar polygons:
$A_1/A_2 = (\text{side}_1/\text{side}_2)^2$

Example problems:

If an interior angle of a regular polygon measures 108°; how many sides does it have?

m $\angle i$ = 108° m $\angle c$ = 180° – m $\angle i$ so m $\angle c$ = 180° – 108° = 72°

m $\angle c$ = 360°/n so 72° = 360°/n n = 5

The areas of similar polygons are 25 and 81 square units. If the length of a side of the larger polygon is 72, what is the length of the corresponding side of the smaller polygon?

A smaller/A larger = $(x/72)^2$ = $\sqrt{\frac{25}{81}} = \frac{x}{72}$; x = 40

Triangles:

The angles in a triangle add up to 180°

Area of a triangle = ½ x b x h or ½bh

Pythagoras' Theorem: $a^2 + b^2 = c^2$

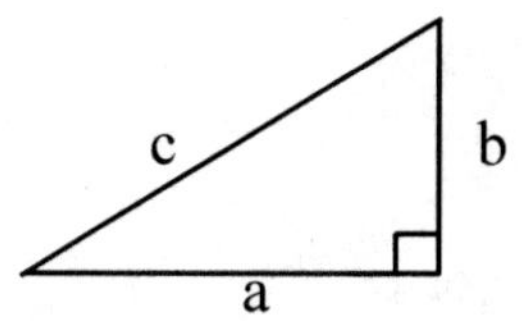

Special triangles

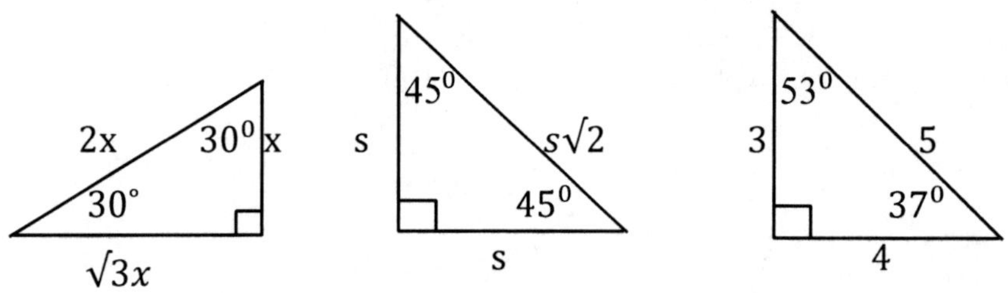

TEST SECRET

Memorizing the values of the special triangles can sometimes eliminate having to make calculations.

Trapezoids:

Four-sided polygon in which the bases (and only the bases) are parallel.
Isosceles Trapezoid – base angles are congruent.

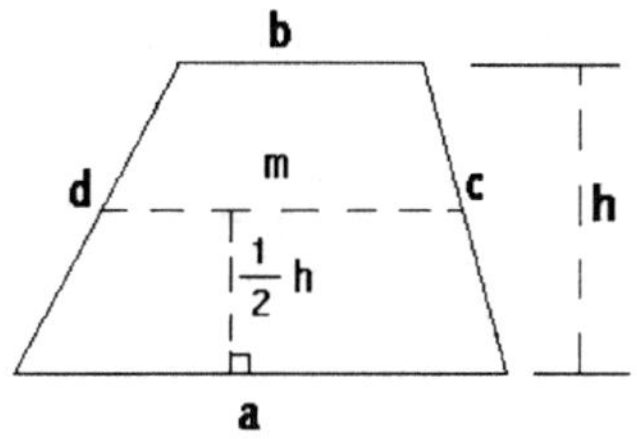

Area and Perimeter of a Trapezoid

$$m = \frac{1}{2}(a+b)$$

$$Area = \frac{1}{2}h\cdot(a+b) = m\cdot h$$

$$Perimeter = a+b+c+d$$
$$= 2m+c+d$$

if m is the median then: $m \parallel \overline{AB}$ and $m \parallel CD$

Example problem:

Find the value of Y of the following trapezoid.

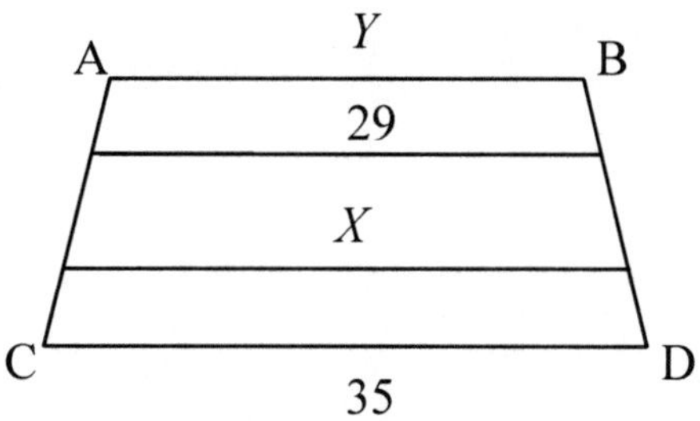

Solution: $X = ½(29 + 35) = 32$ so $29 = ½(32 + Y)$ $Y = 26$

Rhombus:

Four-sided polygon in which all four sides are congruent and opposite sides are parallel.

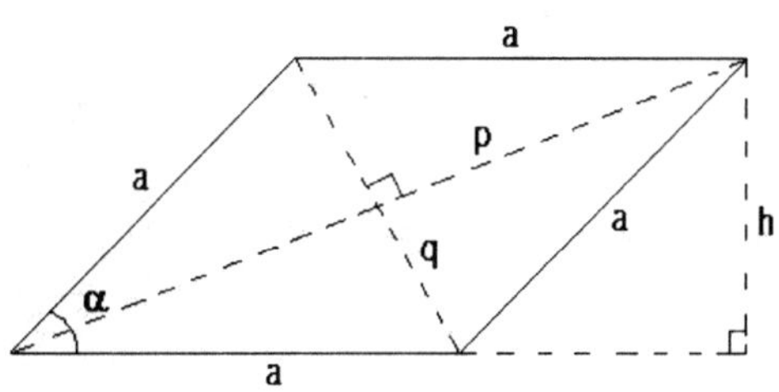

Area and Perimeter of a Rhombus

$$Perimeter = 4a$$

$$Area = a^2 \sin\alpha = a\cdot h = \frac{1}{2}pq$$

$$4a^2 = p^2 + q^2$$

Example problem:

Solve for x and y.

$\overline{AC}$ bisects $\angle A$ so
$4x - 5 = 2x + 15$; $x = 10$
Hence, $2x + 15 = 35$ and
$m\angle A = 2(35) = 70$
Since $\angle A$ and $\angle B$ are supplementary,
$y + 70 = 180$; $y = 110$

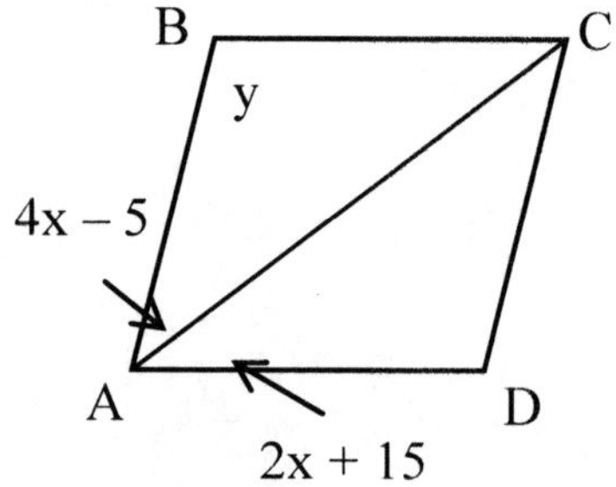

Rectangle:

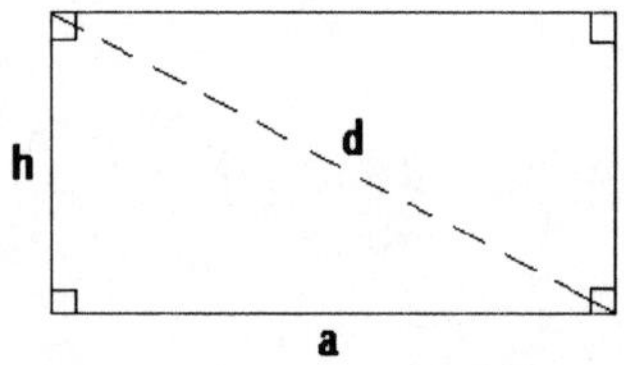

Area and Perimeter of a Rectangle

$d = \sqrt{a^2 + h^2}$

$a = \sqrt{d^2 - h^2}$

$h = \sqrt{d^2 - a^2}$

$Perimeter = 2a + 2h$

Square:

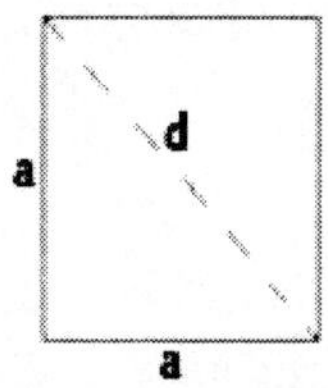

Area and Perimeter of a Square

$d = a\sqrt{2}$

$Perimeter = 4a = 2d\sqrt{2}$

$Area = a^2 = \frac{1}{2}d^2$

Circle:

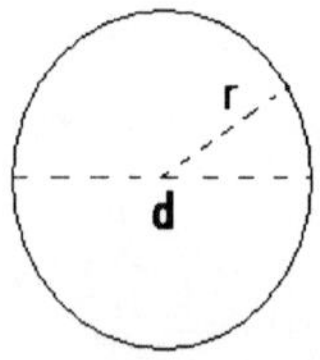

Area and Perimeter of a Circle

$d = 2r$

$Perimeter = 2\pi r = \pi d$

$Area = \pi r^2$

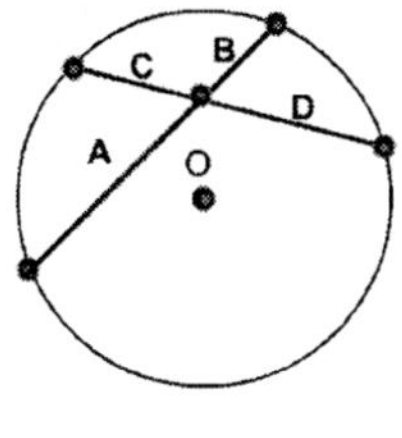

The product length of one chord equals the product length of the other, or:
AB=CD

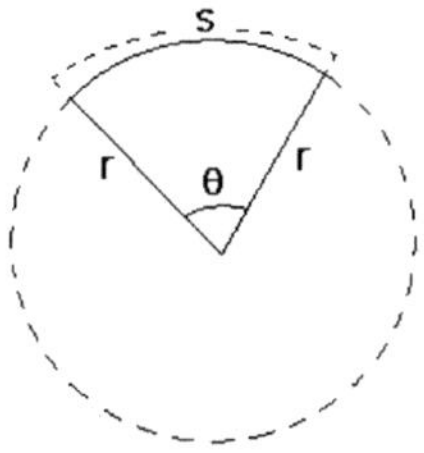

Area and Perimeter of the Sector of a Circle

$$\alpha = \frac{\theta\pi}{180}\ (rad)$$

$$s = r\alpha$$

$$Perimeter = 2r + s$$

$$Area = \frac{1}{2}\theta\, r^2\ (radians)\ or\ \frac{n}{360}\pi r^2$$

$$length\ (l)\ of\ an\ arc\ \ l = \frac{\pi n r}{180}\ or\ \frac{n}{360}\, 2\pi r$$

TEST SECRET

Make sure you review converting degrees and radians. The formula $\alpha = \frac{\theta\pi}{180}$ is used to convert degrees to radians. If the answer is to be given in radians, omit α from the equation.

Overall conversion factors are:
$360^\circ = 2\pi$ radians
$180^\circ = \pi$ radians

Area and Perimeter of the Segment of a Circle

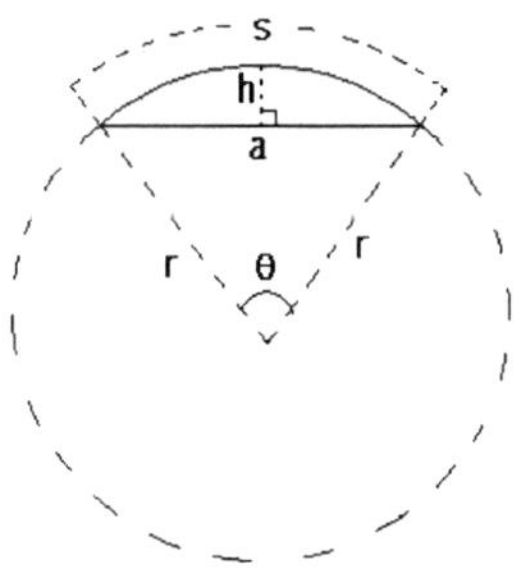

$$\alpha = \frac{\theta\pi}{180}\ (rad)$$

$$a = 2\sqrt{2hr - h^2}$$

$$a^2 = 2r^2 - 2r^2\cos\theta$$

$$s = r\alpha$$

$$h = r - \frac{1}{2}\sqrt{4r^2 - a^2}$$

$$Perimeter = a + s$$

$$Area = \frac{1}{2}[sr - a(r - h)]$$

Example problems:

What is the radius of a circle if a 40° arc has a length of 4π?

$$l = 4\pi \text{ and } n^o = 40, \text{ so:}$$
$$4\pi = \frac{40}{360} 2\pi r$$
$$r = 18$$

Find the area of the sector of a circle (in radians) of radius 5 cm if the central angle of the circle is $\frac{2\pi}{3}$.

Since an angle measurement in radians is given, there is no need to convert. So:

$$A = \frac{1}{2}\theta r^2 \quad A = \frac{1}{2}(5^2)(\frac{2\pi}{3}) = \frac{25\pi}{3}\text{cm}^2$$

TEST SECRET

Make sure to remember your elementary tangent and chord principles.

Cube:

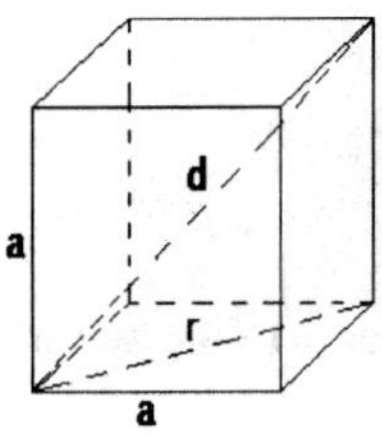

Area and Volume of a Cube

$r = a\sqrt{2}$

$d = a\sqrt{3}$

$Area = 6a^2$

$Volume = a^3$

Cuboid

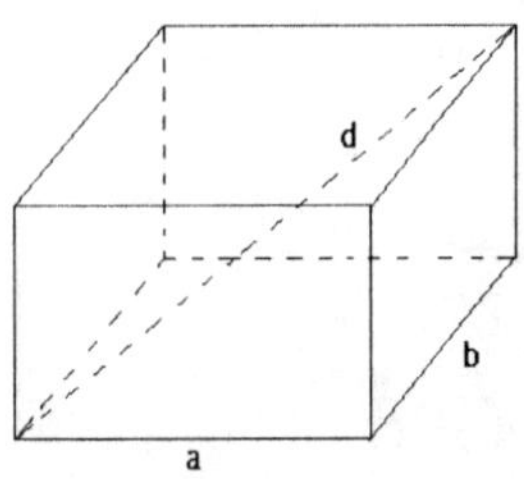

Area and Volume of a Cuboid

$d = \sqrt{a^2 + b^2 + c^2}$

$A = 2(ab + ac + bc)$

$V = abc$

Pyramid:

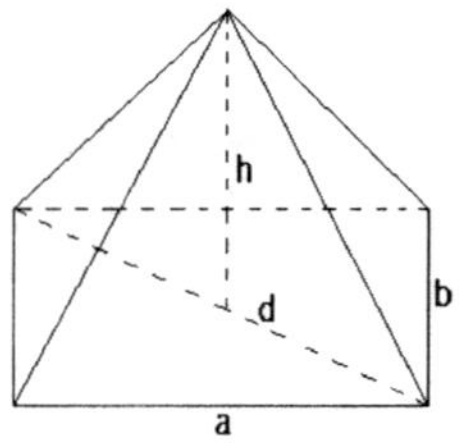

Area and Volume of a Pyramid

$$A_{lateral} = a\sqrt{h^2 + \left(\frac{b}{2}\right)^2} + b\sqrt{h^2 + \left(\frac{a}{2}\right)^2}$$

$$d = \sqrt{a^2 + b^2}$$

$$A_{base} = ab$$

$$A_{total} = A_{lateral} + A_{base}$$

$$V = \frac{1}{3}abh$$

Cylinder:

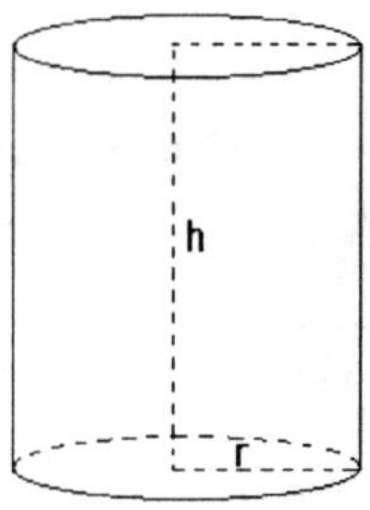

Area and Volume of a Cylinder

$$d = 2r$$

$$A_{surface} = 2\pi rh$$

$$A_{base} = 2\pi r^2$$

$$Area = A_{surface} + A_{base}$$

$$= 2\pi r\,(h + r)$$

$$Volume = \pi r^2 h$$

Cone:

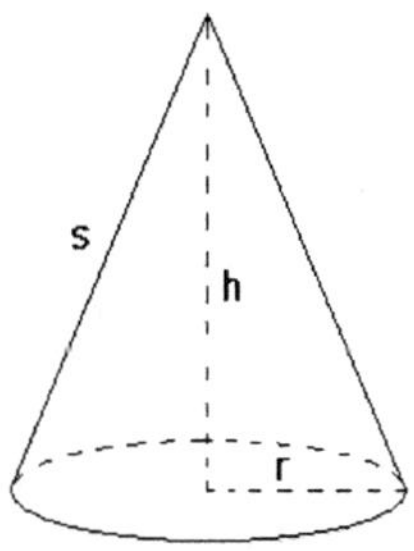

Area and Volume of a Cone

$$d = 2r$$

$$A_{surface} = \pi rs$$

$$A_{base} = \pi r^2$$

$$Area = A_{surface} + A_{base}$$

$$= 2\pi r\,(h + r)$$

$$Volume = \frac{1}{3}\pi r^2 h$$

Sphere:

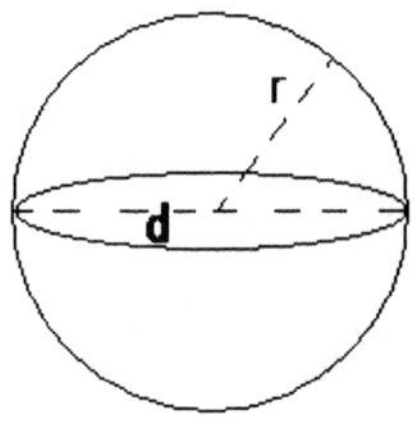

Area and Volume of a Sphere

$d = 2r$

$A_{surface} = 4\pi r^2$

$Volume = \frac{4}{3}\pi r^3$

- Trigonometry

The trigonometry questions on the ACT test basic trigonomic relationships. You should know the following:

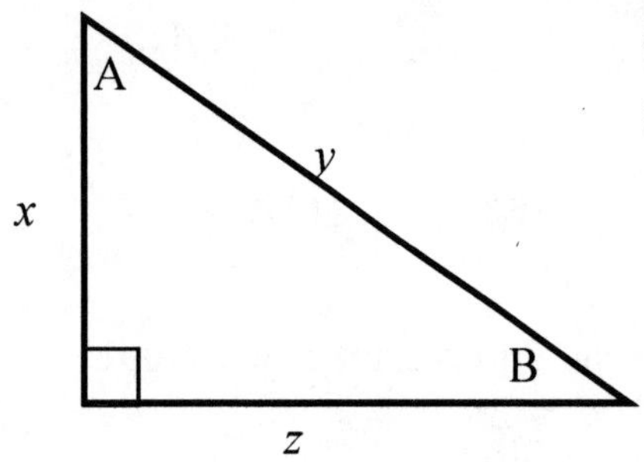

SOH-CAH-TOA

Sine (sin) = **O**pposite/**H**ypotenuse (SOH)
Cosine (cos) = **A**djacent/**H**ypotenuse (CAH)
Tangent (tan) = **O**pposite/**A**djacent (TOA)

sin A = $\frac{z}{y}$ sin B = $\frac{x}{y}$

cos A = $\frac{x}{y}$ cos B = $\frac{z}{y}$

tan A = $\frac{z}{x}$ tan B = $\frac{x}{x}$

tan A = $\frac{1}{\tan B}$ tan B = $\frac{1}{\tan A}$

secant (sec) = $\frac{1}{\cos}$

cosecant (csc) = $\frac{1}{\sin}$

cotangent (tan) = $\frac{1}{\tan}$

Important Identities

$$\sin\alpha \pm \sin\beta = 2\sin\frac{1}{2}(\alpha \pm \beta)\cos\frac{1}{2}(\alpha \mp \beta)$$

$$\cos\alpha + \cos\beta = 2\cos\frac{1}{2}(\alpha + \beta)\cos\frac{1}{2}(\alpha - \beta)$$

$$\sin(a+b) = \sin a\cos b + \cos a\sin b$$
$$\cos(a+b) = \cos a\cos b - \sin a\sin b$$
$$\sin(a-b) = \sin a\cos b - \cos a\sin b$$
$$\cos(a-b) = \cos a\cos b + \sin a\sin b$$

$\sin^2\theta + \cos^2\theta = 1$
$1 + \tan^2\theta = \sec^2\theta$
$1 + \cot^2\theta = \csc^2\theta$

$\sin(-\theta) = -\sin\theta$ $\csc(-\theta) = -\csc\theta$
$\cos(-\theta) = \cos\theta$ $\sec(-\theta) = \sec\theta$
$\tan(-\theta) = -\tan\theta$ $\cot(-\theta) = -\cot\theta$

Double Angle Formulas

$\sin 2\theta = 2\sin\theta\cos\theta$
$\cos 2\theta = \cos^2\theta - \sin^2\theta = 1 - 2\sin^2\theta = 2\cos^2\theta - 1$

Tangent-slope theorem

$m = \tan\theta$

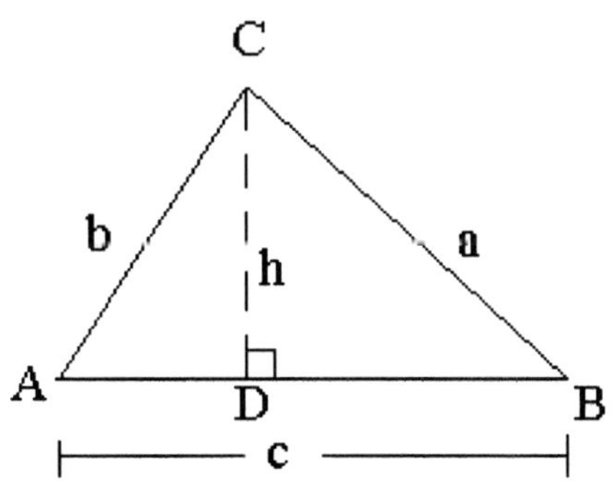

Law of Sines: SinA/a = SinB/b = SinC/c

Law of Cosines:

$a^2 = b^2 + c^2 - 2bc\cos A$
$b^2 = a^2 + c^2 - 2ac\cos B$

$c^2 = a^2 + b^2 - 2ab\text{Cos}C$

To find an angle in the triangle when given three sides, it is easier to switch around the equations and use:

$$\text{Cos}A = (b^2 + c^2 - a^2)/2bc$$
$$\text{Cos}B = (a^2 + c^2 - b^2)/2ac$$
$$\text{Cos}C = (a^2 + b^2 - c^2)/2ab$$

Example problem:

In ΔABC, the $m\angle A = 30^{\circ}$, $\overline{AB} = 8$, and $\overline{BC} = 5$. What is $m\angle C$?

Step 1: Draw it out.

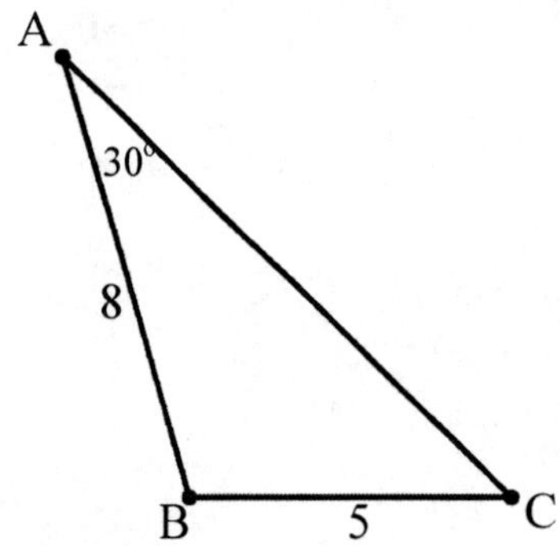

Step 2: Use the Law of Sines

$\sin 30^{o}/5 = \sin C/8$

$8 \sin 30/5 = \sin c$

Supplements Theorem: (for every θ)

radians: $\sin(\pi - \theta) = \sin\theta$
$\cos(\pi - \theta) = -\cos\theta$
$\tan(\pi - \theta) = -\tan\theta$

degrees: $\sin(180 - \theta) = \sin\theta$
$\cos(180 - \theta) = -\cos\theta$
$\tan(180 - \theta) = -\tan\theta$

Complements Theorem: (for every θ)

radians: $\sin(\pi/2 - \theta) = \cos\theta$
$\cos(\pi/2 - \theta) = \sin\theta$

degrees: $\sin(90 - \theta) = \cos\theta$
$\cos(90 - \theta) = \sin\theta$

Example problem:

If $\cos \theta = 3/5$, find $\sin \theta$.

$$\sin^2\theta + \cos^2\theta = 1$$

$$\sin^2\theta + \left(\frac{3}{5}\right)^2 = 1$$

$$\sin^2\theta + \frac{9}{25} = 1 \qquad \sin^2\theta = \frac{16}{25} \qquad \sin\theta = \sqrt{\frac{16}{25}} \qquad \sin\theta = \pm\frac{4}{5}$$

Trigonomic graphs:

You will need to know the following basic trigonomic graphs and the unit circle:

Unit Circle

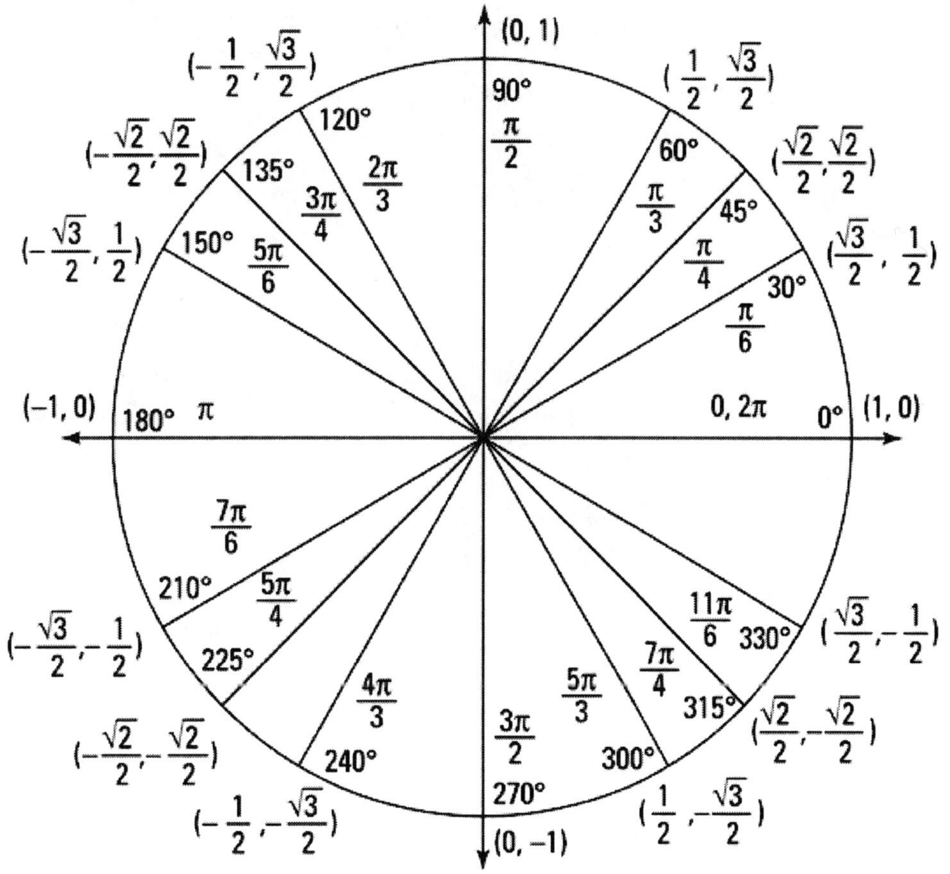

Sine

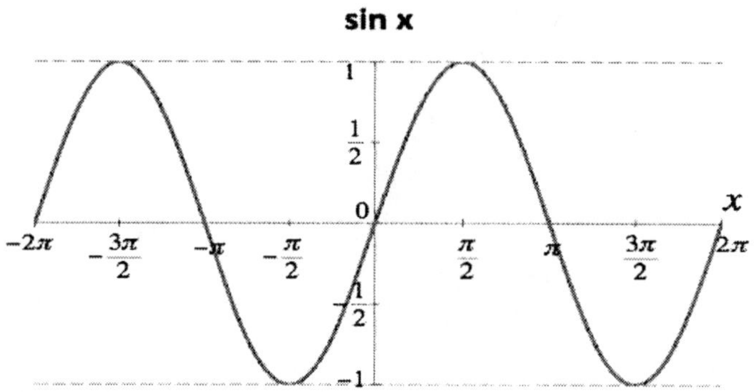

Period: $2\boldsymbol{\pi}$
Domain: All real numbers
Range: {y: -1 ≤ y ≤ 1}
y intercept: 0
x intercept: Integral multiples of $\boldsymbol{\pi}$ (…-2$\boldsymbol{\pi}$, -$\boldsymbol{\pi}$, 0, $\boldsymbol{\pi}$,…)

Cosine

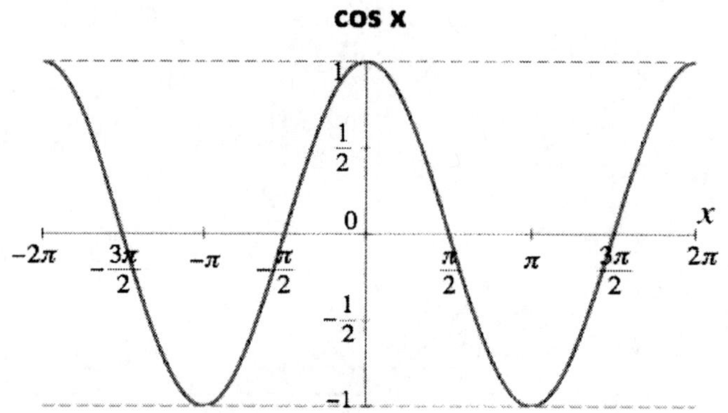

Period: $2\boldsymbol{\pi}$
Domain: All real numbers
Range: {y: -1 ≤ y ≤ 1}
y intercept: 1
x intercept: Odd multiples of $\boldsymbol{\pi}$/2 (…-$\boldsymbol{\pi}$/2, $\boldsymbol{\pi}$/2, 3$\boldsymbol{\pi}$/3, …)

Tangent

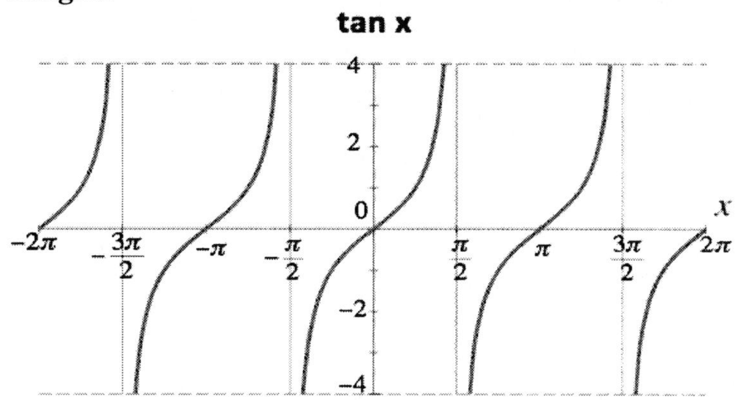

Period: π
Domain: All real numbers except odd multiples of $\pi/2$
Range: All real numbers
y intercept: No min or max value
x intercept: Multiples of π ($\ldots -\pi, 0, \pi, 2\pi, \ldots$)
$\log_b x = y$ $\quad\quad b^y = x$
$\log_b(xy) = \log_b x + \log_b y$
$\log_b(x/y) = \log_b x - \log_b y$
$\log_b(x^n) = n\log_b x$
$\log_b(\sqrt[k]{A}) = 1/k \log A$
change of base: $\quad \log_b a = \log_c a / \log_c b$

Example problem:

Evaluate $\log_3(81 \cdot 9)$

$\log_3 81 + \log_3 9$
$3^x = 81$ and $3^y = 9$
$x = 4$ and $y = 2$
$4 + 2 = 6$

For more help on Trigonometry, see Section11 of the Math Question Bank.

- Fundamental Counting Principle

The number of possibilities of an event happening times the number of possibilities of another event happening = the total number of possibilities

Example:

If you take a multiple choice test with 5 questions, with 4 answer choices for each question, how many test result possibilities are there?

Solution:

Question 1 has 4 choices, question 2 has 4 choices, etc., so you have 4*4*4*4*4 (one for each question) = 1024 possible test results.

For more help on Fundamental Counting Principle, see Section 9 of the Math Question Bank.

- Permutations

The number of ways a set number of items can be arranged, recognized by the use of a factorial ($n!$), with n being the number of items. If n=3, then $3! = 3*2*1 = 6$. If you need to arrange n number of things, but x number are alike, then $n!$ is divided by $x!$

Example:

How many different ways can the letters in the word **balance** be arranged?

Solution:

There are 7 letters so $n! = 7!$ and 2 letters are the same so $x! = 2!$ Set up the equation:

$$\frac{7 \times 6 \times 5 \times 4 \times 3 \times 2 \times 1}{2 \times 1} = 2540 \text{ ways}$$

For more help on Permutations, see Section 9 of the Math Question Bank.

- Combinations

To calculate the total number of possible combinations, use the formula: $n!/r!\,(n-r)!$ n = # of objects r = # of objects selected at a time

Example:
If seven people are selected in groups of three, how many different combinations are possible?

Solution:

$$\frac{(7 \, x \, 6 \, x \, 5 \, x \, 4 \, x \, 3 \, x \, 2 \, x \, 1)}{(3x2 \, x \, 1)(7-3)} = 210 \text{ possible combinations}$$

For more help on Combinations, see Section 9 of the Math Question Bank.

- Probabilities

Number of desired outcomes / Number of possible outcomes
(the piece / the whole)

For more help on Probabilities, see Section 10 of the Math Question Bank.

Chapter 6: The English Section

The English portion of the ACT contains five passages of which you will answer two categories of questions: rhetorical, and usage/mechanics. There are only 45 minutes to answer 75 questions. You will receive three scores, one for each category, and an overall score. The following is a description of the types of questions found in each category, with the number of corresponding questions found on the test in parentheses.

The **usage/mechanics questions** coordinate with numbered, underlined words or phrases and cover the following concepts:

- **Punctuation (14%):** Apostrophes, colons, semi-colons, commas, dashes, hyphens, quotation marks, parentheses, and their function in clarifying the meaning of the text selection.

- **Basic Grammar (16%):** Verbs, adverbs, adjectives, subject-verb agreement,pronoun-antecedent agreement, and proper use of connectives.

- **Sentence Structure (24%):** Clauses, modifiers, parallelism, consistency in tense and point of view.

The **rhetorical questions** are based on either parts of passage or its entirety:

- **Strategy (16%):** The author's choice of supporting material – if is it effective, applicable, and ample in quality and quantity.

- **Style (16%):** The best choice of adjectives, word order, or alternative wording that most concisely articulates an idea.

- **Organization (14%):** Sentence arrangement within a paragraph, paragraph arrangement within the passage, the need for further information, and the presence of unnecessary information.

English Section Tips

Remember, this is a knowledge-based test, not a reasoning exam. As with all the section tests, you have to know your English grammar. The ACT is not unjustly 'sneaky,' but you have to be observant and thorough enough to catch the errors. Here are some tips to help improve your score.

The three main No-No's.

There are three main things the ACT is stringent about:

1. **Redundancy** (repetitious text or words).

2. **Irrelevance** (words or ideas not directly or logically associated with the purpose or main idea).

3. **Wordiness** (drawing out a sentence).

Eliminate anything that isn't pertinent and necessary to the meaning of the passage. The writers of the ACT consider the best choice one which is clear-cut and concise, using the least number of words possible while still applying proper English.

Peruse the entire passage paragraph before answering any of the questions.

Many ACT guides will tell you not to read the entire passage before answering the usage/mechanics questions; however, that approach lends to a greater possibility of error. The overall meaning or purpose of the paragraph can change the propriety of the highlighted text. For example, looking at just the sentence containing the highlighted word group may cause you to misinterpret the intended parallels or point of view.

Read every word of every question.

Don't assume you know what is being asked after reading the first few words. Remember, one word at the end of a sentence can change its entire meaning.

Read all the answer choices before making a selection.

Some choices will be partially correct (pertaining to a part, but not all, of the passage) and are intended to catch the eye of the sloppy tester. Note the differences between your answer choices; sometimes they are very subtle.

Understand transitions.
The ACT will require you to recognize the shortest, most proper way to go from one sentence or paragraph to another.

Familiarize yourself with various styles of writing.
The ACT passages can be poetry, cause/effect essays, comparison /contrast essays, definition essays, description essays, narration essays, persuasive essays, or process analysis essays.

Learn the directions.
Knowing the directions before test day saves valuable minutes. It enables you to glance quickly at the directions and start answering questions.

Standard Directions for the English Section:
This test consists of five passages. In each passage, certain words and phrases have been underlined and numbered. The questions on each passage consist of alternatives for these underlined segments. Choose the alternative that follows standard written English, most accurately reflects the style and tone of the passage, or best relays the idea of the passage. Choose "No Change" if no change is necessary. You are to choose the best answer to the question.

You will also find questions about a section of the passage, or the passage as a whole. These questions do not refer to the underlined portions of the passage, but are identified by a boxed number. For each question, choose the alternative that best answers the question.

TEST SECRET

Practice, Practice, Practice! There is no magic bullet to improving on the English section of the ACT. The more you practice these types of questions and take a couple practice exams, the more familiar you will become with the types of questions asked. This will not only help relieve test anxiety, but help you improve your score.

Test Your Knowledge – English Section

A Voice of Her Own

Sandra Cisneros, perhaps the best known Latina author in the United States, [1] writes poems and stories whose titles alone – "Barbie-Q", "My Lucy Friend Who Smells Like Corn", "Woman Hollering Creek" – engage potential readers' [2] curiosity.

1.

A) NO CHANGE
B) author and writer
C) author and novelist
D) wordsmith and author

2.

F) NO CHANGE
G) potential, reader's
H) potential, readers
J) potential readers

Ironically, this renowned writer, whose books are printed on recycled paper, [3] did not do well in school. When she lectures at schools and public libraries, Cisneros presents the evidence. [4] An elementary school report card containing Cs, Ds and a solitary B (for conduct). Cisneros has a theory to explain her low grades: teachers had low expectations for Latina and Latino students from Chicago's South Side.

3.

A) NO CHANGE
B) writer, who is recognized by her orange and black eyeglasses
C) writer, who likes to write at night,
D) writer

4.

F) NO CHANGE
G) evidence: an
H) evidence; an
J) evidence an

Despite the obstacles that she faced in school, Cisneros completed not only high school but also college. Her persistence paid off in her twenties, when Cisneros was admitted prestigious to the Writers' Workshop

5

at the University of Iowa.

5.

The best placement for the underlined portion would be:

A) Where it is now.
B) Before the word admitted.
C) Before the word Writers'.
D) Before the word Workshop.

Cisneros soon observed that most of

6

her classmates at the university seemed to have a common set of memories, based on middle-class childhoods, from which to draw in their writing.

6.

F) NO CHANGE
G) furthermore
H) nevertheless
J) therefore

Cisneros felt

7

7.

A) NO CHANGE
B) Cisneros herself,
C) Cisneros, herself
D) Cisneros,

decided out of place.

8

8.

F) NO CHANGE
G) deciding
H) decidedly
J) decidedly and

9

9.
Which of the following true statements, if added here, would best serve as a transition between the challenges Cisneros faced as an aspiring writer and her success in meeting those challenges?

A) She did not know what to do.
B) Then she had a break through.
C) At that point she almost went home to Chicago.
D) She wondered whether she was in the right field.

She decided to speak from her own experience. Her voice, which by being one of a Latina living outside of the mainstream,
10
found a large and attentive audience in

10.

F) NO CHANGE
G) voice – that of a Latina living outside the mainstream –
H) voice, being one of a Latina living outside the mainstream, it
J) voice – in which it was a Latina living outside the mainstream –

1984 with the publication of her first short
11
story collection, *The House on Mango Street.*

11.

A) NO CHANGE
B) 1984, With
C) 1984; with
D) 1984, with,

Today the book is read by middle
12
school, high school, and college students across the United States.

12.

F) NO CHANGE
G) In the future,
H) Meanwhile,
J) At the same time,

Cisneros uses her influence as a successful writer to help other Latina and

Latino writers get their works published. But <u>having made the argument that,</u> 13 in order for large numbers of young Latinos to achieve literary success, the educational system itself must change. Cisneros <u>hints</u> 14 that she succeeded in spite of the educational system. "I'm the exception," she insists, "not the rule." [15]

13.
A) NO CHANGE
B) she argues that,
C) arguing that,
D) she argues that, when

14.
Which choice best shows that Cisneros is emphatic about expressing the belief stated in this sentence?
F) NO CHANGE
G) Says
H) Supposes
J) Asserts

15.
The writer is considering deleting the previous sentence. If the writer decided to delete this sentence, the paragraph would primarily lose a statement that:
A) Enhances the subject and setting.
B) Provides support for a point previously made.
C) Humorously digresses from the main topic of the paragraph.
D) Contradicts Cisneros's claim made earlier in the essay.

Test Your Knowledge Answers – English Section

1. **A)**
2. **F)**
3. **D)**
4. **G)**
5. **C)**
6. **F)**
7. **A)**
8. **H)**
9. **B)**
10. **G)**
11. **A)**
12. **F)**
13. **B)**
14. **J)**
15. **B)**

Chapter 7: The Writing Section

Individuals who choose to take the optional Writing Test will receive two additional ACT sub-test scores: one for the writing test and one that combines both the English and Writing subtest scores, the English subtest counting for 75% of the score. The combined score is then ranked on a 1 (lowest) – 36 scale. The writing score is determined as follows:

The essay is read by two English composition professionals, each giving a grade on a scale of 1 – 6 with 1 being the lowest. Your overall sub-score will range from 2 – 12. Grading is based on how well the student understood the prompt, developed and organized their ideas, and their proper use of the English language. Length of the essay is not important, so using long, wordy sentences or repetition to lengthen a paragraph will hurt you more than help you. Only write enough to support your arguments and nothing more. You will receive a comment on your essay from one of the scorers. Your essay will be available to your high school and the colleges you have chosen to report your scores from that test date.

- **Write plainly:** If they can't read your writing - they can't grade it.

- **Write accurately:** Be sure to stay in the same tense throughout the essay. Pay attention to punctuation, sentence structure, and spelling.

- **Make your point and support it:** Make sure you understand the topic and what is being asked. Take the position on the topic in which you can think of at least two specific examples, including personal experiences.

TEST SECRET

When asked to choose a side on an issue for an essay prompt, it does not matter what side you take. The graders don't care which argument you choose, only that your essay is well written, well supported, and well organized. There is no "right" or "wrong" choice. Just focus on following the three guidelines above!

Tips from the Test Makers

The Writing Section is by nature a very subjective section, since it is not a multiple choice and there is no obvious correct or incorrect answer. Take note of the tips given by the test makers, because you know they will expect you to know this at a minimum:

- Do some planning before writing the essay; you will be instructed to do your prewriting in your Writing Test booklet. You can refer to these notes as you write the essay on the lined pages in your answer folder.

- Do not skip lines and do not write in the margins. Write your essay legibly, in English, with a No. 2 pencil. Do not use ink, a mechanical pencil, or correction fluid.
- Carefully consider the prompt and make sure you understand the issue – reread it if you aren't sure.
- Decide what perspective you want to take on the issue.
- Jot down your ideas. This may simply be a list of reasons and examples that you will use to explain your point of view on the issue.
- Write down what you think others might say in opposition to your point of view and think about how you would refute their arguments.
- Think of how best to organize your essay.
- At the beginning of your essay, make sure readers will see that you understand the issue. Explain your point of view in a clear and logical way.
- Stay focused on the topic.
- Discuss the issue in a broader context, or evaluate the implications or complications of the issue.
- Address what others might say to refute your point of view and present a counterargument.
- Use specific examples.
- Vary the structure of your sentences, and use varied and precise word choices.
- Make logical relationships clear by using transitional words and phrases.
- End with a strong conclusion that summarizes or reinforces your position.
- If possible, before time is called, recheck your work:
    - Correct any mistakes in grammar, usage, punctuation, and spelling.
    - If you find any words that are hard to read, recopy them so your readers can read them easily.
    - Make any corrections and revisions neatly, between the lines (but not in the margins).[1]

[1]Information found at www.actstudent.org

Instructions

As always, you should already know the instructions before sitting down for the exam.

Directions for the Writing Section:

This is a test of your writing skills. You will have thirty (30) minutes to write an essay in English. Before you begin planning and writing your essay, read the writing prompt carefully to understand exactly what you are being asked to do. Your essay will be evaluated on the evidence it provides of your ability to express judgments by taking a position on the issue in the writing prompt; to maintain a focus on the topic throughout the essay; to develop a position by using logical reasoning and by supporting your ideas; to organize ideas in a logical way; and to use language clearly and effectively according to the conventions of standard written English.

You may use the unlined pages in this test booklet to plan your essay. These pages will not be scored. ***You must write your essay in pencil on the lined pages in the answer folder****. Your writing on those lined pages will be scored. You may not need all the lined pages, but to ensure you have enough room to finish, do NOT skip lines. You may write corrections or additions neatly between the lines of your essay, but do NOT write in the margins of the lined pages.* ***Illegible essays cannot be scored, so you must write (or print) clearly.***

If you finish before time is called, you may review your work. Lay your pencil down immediately when time is called.

DO NOT OPEN THIS BOOKLET UNTIL YOU ARE TOLD TO DO SO.

Essay Examples and Evaluations:

Prompt:

Research tells us that what children learn in their earliest years is very important to their future success in school. Because of this, public schools all over the country are starting to offer Pre-Kindergarten classes.

What are the benefits of starting school early? What are some of the problems you see in sending four-year-olds to school?

Write a composition in which you weigh the pros and cons of public school education for Pre-Kindergartners. Give reasons and specific examples to support your opinion. There is no specific word limit for your composition, but it should be long enough to give a clear and complete presentation of your ideas.

Sample Score 4+ Essay

Today, more and more four-year-olds are joining their big brothers and sisters on the school bus and going to Pre-Kindergarten. Although the benefits of starting school early are clear, it is also clear that Pre-K is not for every child.

The students who are successful in Pre-K are ahead when they start kindergarten. Pre-K teaches them to play well with others. Even though it does not teach skills like reading and writing, it does help to prepare students for "real" school. Pre-K students sing songs, dance, paint and draw, climb and run. They learn to share and to follow directions. They tell stories and answer questions, and as they do, they add new words to their vocabularies. Pre-K can also give students experiences they might not get at home. They might take trips to the zoo or the farm, have visits from musicians or scientists, and so on. These experiences help the students better understand the world.

There are, however, some real differences among children of this age. Some four-year-olds are just not ready for the structure of school life. Some have a hard time leaving home, even for only three or four hours a day. Other children may already be getting a great preschool education at home or in daycare.

While you weigh the advantages and disadvantages of Pre-K, it is safe to say that each child is different. For some children, it is a wonderful introduction to the world of school. But others may not or should not be forced to attend Pre-K.

Evaluation of Sample Score 4+ Essay:

This paper is clearly organized and has stated a definite point of view. The paper opens with an introduction and closes with a conclusion. The introduction and conclusion combine an expression of the writer's opinion. Connections to the writer's opinion are made throughout the paper.

Sample Score 3 Essay

Just like everything in life, there are pros and cons to early childhood education. Pre-K classes work for many children, but they aren't for everyone. The plusses of Pre-K are obvious. Pre-K children learn many skills that will help them in kindergarten and later on. Probably the most important thing they learn is how to follow directions. This is a skill they will need at all stages of their life.

Other plusses include simple tasks like cutting, coloring in the lines, and learning capital letters. Many children don't get these skills at home. They need Pre-K to prepare them for kindergarten.

The minuses of Pre-K are not as obvious, but they are real. Children at this young age need the comfort of home. They need to spend time with parents, not strangers. They need that security. If parents are able to, they can give children the background they need to do well in school.

Other minuses include the fact that a lot of four year-old children can't handle school. They don't have the maturaty to sit still, pay attention, or share with others. Given another year, they may mature enough to do just fine in school. Sometimes it's better just to wait.

So there are definitely good things about Pre-K programs in our public schools, and I would definitely want to see one in our local schools. However, I think parents should decide whether their children are ready for a Pre-K education or not.

Evaluation of Sample Score 3 Essay:

This paper has an identifiable organization plan, with pros and cons listed in order. The development is easy to understand, if not somewhat simplistic. The language of the paper is uneven, with some vague turns of phrase: "Just like everything in life," "definitely some good things." The word "maturity" is also misspelled. However, the essay is clear and controlled, and generally follows written conventions. If the writer had included more developed and explicit examples and used more varied words, this paper might have earned a higher score.

Sample Score 2 Essay

Is early childhood education a good idea? It depends on the child you're talking about. Some children probally need more education in the early years and need something to do to keep out of trouble. Like if there isnt any good nursry school or day care around it could be very good to have Pre-Kindergarten at the school so those children could have a good start on life. A lot of skills could be learned in Pre-Kindergarten, for example they could learn to write their name, cut paper, do art, etc.

Of course theres some kids who wouldnt do well, acting out and so on, so they might do better staying home than going to Pre-Kindergarten, because they just arent ready for school, and maybe wouldn't even be ready for kindergarten the next year either. Some kids just act younger than others or are too baby-ish for school.

So I would suport Pre-Kindergarten in our schools, it seems like a good idea to have someplace for those kids to go. Even if some kids wouldnt do well I think enough kids would do well, and it would make a diference in their grades as they got older. All those skills that they learned would help them in the future. If we did have Pre-Kindergarten it would help their working parents too, knowing their kids were someplace safe and learning importent things for life.

Evaluation of Sample Score 2 Essay:

Although the writer of this paper has some good points to make, a lack of language skills, considerable misspellings, and a certain disconnectedness of thought keep the paper from scoring high. The paper begins with a vague introduction of the topic and ends with a paragraph that expresses the author's opinion, but the rest of the paper is disorganized. The reasons given do not always have examples to support them, and the examples that are given are weak.

Sample Score 1 Essay

What are benefits? What are some of problems with sending four-year-olds to school? Well, for one problem, its hard to see how little kids would do with all those big kids around at the school. They might get bullyed or lern bad habits, so I wouldnt want my four year old around those big kids on the bus and so on. Its hard to see how that could be good for a four year old. In our area we do have Pre-Kindergarten at our school but you dont have to go there a lot of kids in the program, I think about 50 or more, you see them a lot on the play ground mostly all you see them do is play around so its hard to see how that could be too usefull. They could play around at home just as easy. A reason for not doing Pre-Kindergarten is then what do you learn in Kindergarten. Why go do the same thing two years when you could just do one year when your a little bit bigger (older). I wonder do the people who want Pre-Kindergarten just want there kids out of the house or a baby sitter for there kids. Its hard to see why do we have to pay for that. I dont even know if Kindergarten is so usefull anyway, not like first grade where you actially learn something. So I would say theres lots of problems with Pre-Kindergarten.

Evaluation of Sample Score 1 Essay:

This paper barely responds to the prompt. It gives reasons not to support Pre-K instruction, but it does not present any benefits of starting school early. The writer repeats certain phrases ("It's hard to see") to no real effect, and the faulty spelling, grammar, and punctuation significantly impede understanding. Several sentences wander off the topic entirely ("there a lot of kids in the program, I think about 50 or more, you see them a lot on the playground.", "I dont even know if Kindergarten is so usefull anyway, not like first grade where you actially learn something."). Instead of opening with an introduction, the writer simply lifts phrases from the prompt. The conclusion states the writer's opinion, but the reasons behind it are illogical and vague. Rather than organizing the essay in paragraph form, the writer has written a single, run-on paragraph. The lack of organization, weak language skills, and failure to address the prompt earn this essay a 1.

Chapter 8: Science Section Question Bank

Each of the seven passages in this test is followed by several questions. After you read each passage, select the correct choice for each of the questions that follow the passage. Refer to the passage as often as necessary to answer the questions. You may NOT use a calculator on this test.

Passage 1

The acceleration of gravity, *g*, is commonly accepted to be 9.8 m/s^2. This means that for every second that an object falls toward the ground, absent any air resistance, it will fall at a velocity 9.8 meters/second faster than the second before. The algebraic equation for acceleration is a= mv^2: acceleration = (mass) times (velocity squared). Two physics students are testing the acceleration of gravity against the commonly accepted value 9.8 by using a Behr free-fall apparatus, shown in Figure 1.

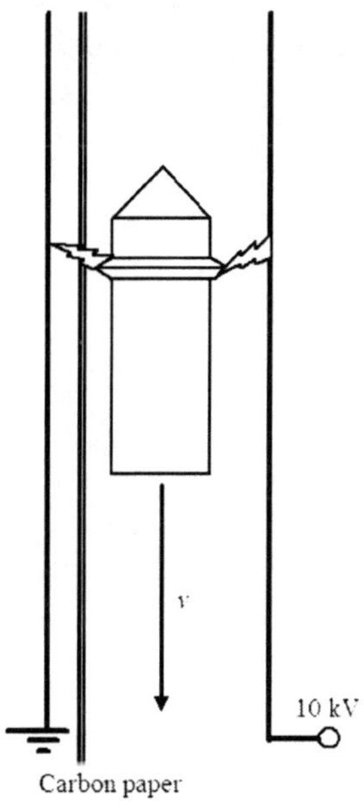

The apparatus has an electromagnet suspended in air between a conducting rod and a grounded wire. The conducting rod is connected to a 10 kV energy supply which is set to turn on momentarily every 1/60th of a second. When this happens, the electromagnet produces a spark.

The students affix a strip of carbon paper between the electromagnet and the grounded wire. As the magnet falls, when the power supply pulses on, the magnet's spark is recorded on this carbon paper. Therefore, the students know that a spark mark is recorded on the paper every 1/60th of a second.

The students set the apparatus up and run it, which produces a strip of carbon paper two meters long with a series of spark marks along it.

Figure 1: Source: Appalachian State University, Physics Dept.

The students record the positions of the first seven spark marks in Table 1, and then they calculate the velocity of the electromagnet at each spark position by finding the difference between the current marking position and the previous spark mark, then dividing this difference by the time interval between the two positions to calculate the average velocity. Since all spark marks were created 1/60th of a second apart, the difference between the positions is divided by 1/60th to find these velocities.

Table 1			
Spark Number	Time	Spark Position	Velocity of magnet
0	0.000 seconds	0.000 meters	---
1	0.033 seconds	0.047 meters	1.53 m/s
2	0.066 seconds	0.102 meters	1.80 m/s
3	0.100 seconds	0.167 meters	2.12 m/s
4	0.133 seconds	0.243 meters	2.48 m/s
5	0.166 seconds	0.431 meters	2.82 m/s
6	0.200 seconds	0.541 meters	3.14 m/s
7	0.233 seconds	0.662 meters	3.47 m/s

The students then graph these spark positions, with time on the x-axis and velocity on the y-axis.

The students exclude the first point on the graph, and find the slope of the line from the second to the seventh points. The slope they found is 10, which is very close to the 9.8 expected from the gravity constant.

Next, the students swap out the electromagnet in the Behr free-fall apparatus for a different electromagnet which weighs 15 grams more than the first one. They re-run the experiment, and record the following positions for the first seven spark marks from this trial in Table 2.

Table 2		
Spark Number	Time	Spark Position
0	0.000 seconds	0.000 meters
1	0.033 seconds	0.042 meters
2	0.066 seconds	0.100 meters
3	0.100 seconds	0.168 meters
4	0.133 seconds	0.243 meters
5	0.166 seconds	0.435 meters
6	0.200 seconds	0.541 meters
7	0.233 seconds	0.660 meters

1. When the students examine the strip of carbon paper with the spark marks on it, how should they expect the spark marks to appear?

A) The marks should be spaced evenly from one another down the length of the paper.
B) The marks should cluster closer together near the bottom of the paper, close to the ground.
C) The marks should be clustered close together near the top, and then spread farther apart near the ground.
D) The sparks should zigzag from right to left across the paper.

2. The students calculated a gravity acceleration of 10 m/s^2 based on their experimental data. This is slightly higher than the theoretical accepted value of gravity's acceleration, which is 9.8 m/s^2. Each of the following could be possible sources of error in the experiment EXCEPT:

A) The timing of the power pulse.
B) The measurement of the distance between the spark marks.
C) The effect of gravity.
D) The angle of the Behr apparatus.

3. If the students were to record the position of the ninth spark mark and calculate the velocity of the electromagnet at that position, what is a likely value of that velocity?

A) 2.97 m/s
B) 3.47 m/s
C) 4.10 m/s
D) 5.59 m/s

4. If the apparatus was set up to produce a spark every $1/30^{th}$ of a second, which of the following changes would the students need to make to their experimental approach?

A) The students would need to measure sparks further down the paper, maybe including sparks up to 1.5 meters along.
B) The students would need to calculate their average velocity at each spark position by dividing the difference of the positions by *two times* the time interval of 1/30.
C) The students would need to include more spark positions in their graph.
D) The students would need to graph with velocity along the y-axis and time along the x-axis to make room for the larger time intervals.

5. Which of the following conclusions is best supported by the students' experiment?

A) A power pulse of 10 kV is sufficient to produce a spark mark on carbon paper.
B) An object in free-fall moves at a velocity that is 10 m/s faster each second that it is falling.
C) The acceleration of gravity is negative.
D) Time moves more slowly as an object falls.

6. Based on the data in Table 2, what can the students conclude?

A) The heavier electromagnet fell at a faster overall average velocity than the lighter magnet.
B) The heavier electromagnet accelerated more quickly than the lighter magnet.
C) Both the lighter and heavier electromagnets accelerated with roughly the same magnitude.
D) Velocity is a function of mass.

7. If the students were to graph the relationship between time and distance of the electromagnet from its starting position, which of the following graphs would result?

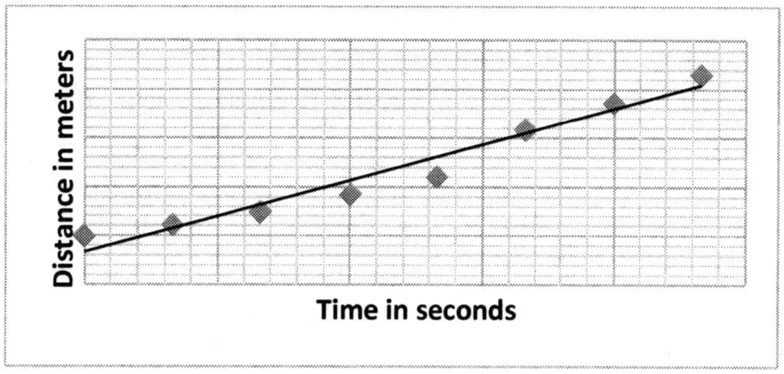

A)

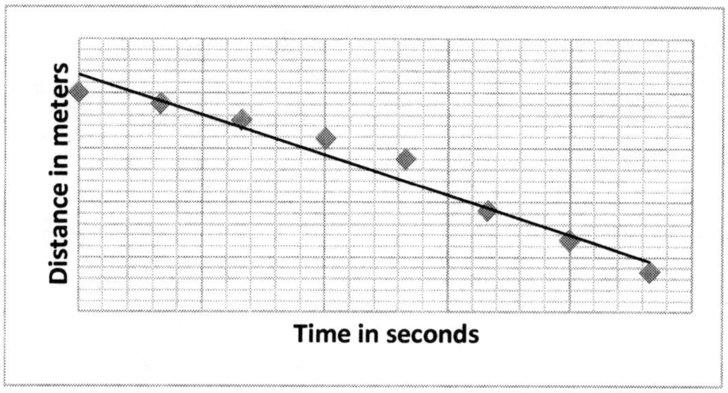

B)

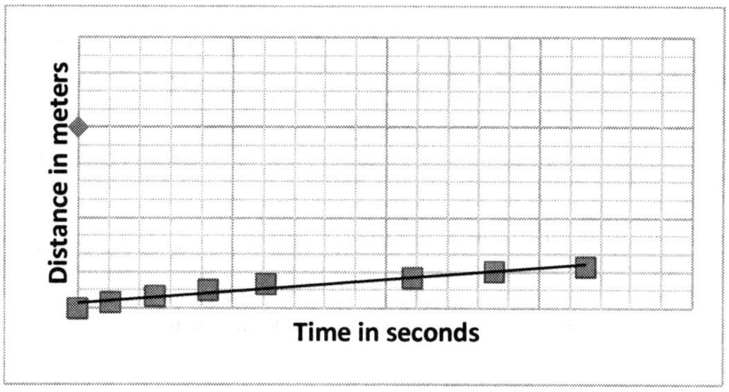

C)

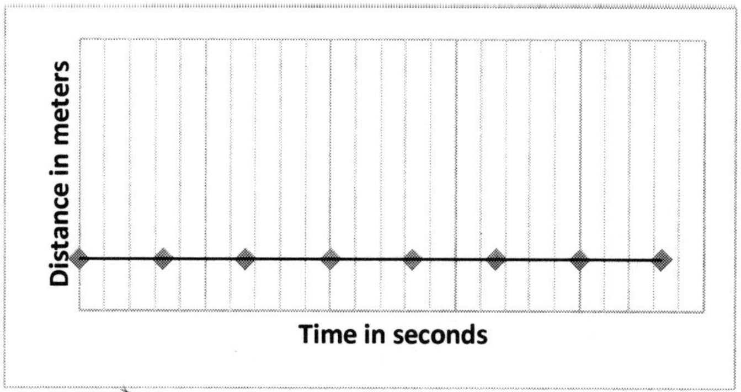

D)

8. This experiment is a more sophisticated version of which of the following experiments?

A) Dropping different objects off of the top of a tall building and recording the time it takes them to land.

B) Bouncing a tennis ball while on a moving platform and having an observer record the overall path of the ball.

C) Rolling a jar down an inclined plane, and then adjusting the steepness of the plane and repeating the test, recording the times for each slope.

D) Calculating the acceleration of an object swinging in a circle, and repeating this for circles of different radii.

9. If astronauts conducted experiment 1 on the surface of the Moon, where the gravitational constant is 1.6 m/s^2 rather than 9.8 m/s^2, how would their results vary from those of these students?

A) The spark marks would be spaced farther apart.

B) The spark marks would be spaced closer together.

C) The spark marks would all be the same distance apart from each other.

D) There would be no difference from the students' results.

Passage 2

In chemistry, the flame test is a way of determining chemical compounds by observing the color of the resulting flame when a chemical reacts to heat. This test works particularly well with substances containing metal ions. An element's atoms, or a compound's molecules, emit a unique spectrum of color when altered to a lower energy state by heat. For example, the element Cu emits blue on the emission spectrum when exposed to heat.

Two students in a chemistry class are doing an experiment using the flame test. The students are given the following chart to complete:

Solution	Flame color
Barium (Ba)	
Calcium (Ca)	
Copper (Cu)	
Lead (Pb)	
Potassium (K)	
Sodium (Na)	
Strontium (Sr)	
Unknown solution #1	
Unknown solution #2	

The students complete the lab procedure. Using a clean test wire, they dip the wire into the first known solution: barium. They then hold the wire in the Bunsen burner flame. The students observe the color that the flame turns and note this on the chart.

The students wait until the chemical burns off of the wire and the flame returns to normal, and then repeat the process for each of the known chemical solutions on the chart. They then test the unknown chemical solutions as well. Below are some of the results the students recorded:

Solution	Flame color
Barium (Ba)	Light green
Calcium (Ca)	Dark red
Copper (Cu)	
Lead (Pb)	White/blue
Potassium (K)	Light purple
Sodium (Na)	Bright orange
Strontium (Sr)	Bright orange/red
Unknown solution #1	
Unknown solution #2	

10. Which of the following colors should the students find the Copper solution emits?

A) Purple
B) White
C) Bright yellow
D) Blue

11. The teacher knows that Unknown solution #2 is simply a Barium solution. What color should students record in their flame charts for Unknown solution #2 to receive full credit?

A) Light green
B) Blue
C) Bright red
D) Bright orange

12. The flame test may not be a useful way to determine a chemical solution for all of the following reasons except that:

A) Some solutions emit similar colors on the spectrum and are hard to distinguish.
B) It might be more difficult to determine the identity of a mixed solution.
C) A contained flame is not always available.
D) The color emitted by different chemicals can change over time.

13. The lab instructor informs the students that they have filled in the wrong color for Strontium – the solution is supposed to be orange, not an orange/red. Which of the following is likely the source of the students' error?

A) The students are both unable to distinguish between red and orange.
B) The students accidentally switched two of the test tubes containing their solutions.
C) The students failed to let all of the Sodium solution burn off while testing the previous solution, so the test wire had both solutions on it.
D) The students misread the solution names on the chart.

14. The students find that Unknown solution #1 is white/blue. Which of the following is the likely metal compound in the solution?

A) Barium
B) Calcium
C) Copper
D) Lead

15. The students learn that fireworks emit bright colors through the use of different chemical compounds. If a fireworks producer wanted to create a red firework, which of the following metals should be added to the compound?

A) Lead
B) Calcium
C) Copper
D) Potassium

16. What color flame would the students expect to record if they dipped a test wire in a solution containing an alloy of Cu and Pb?

A) Light blue
B) Dark blue
C) White
D) Purple

17. Scientists have used the unique color spectrum of elements to determine new elements. The discoveries of each of the following elements illustrates this strategy EXCEPT:

A) The discovery of Radium in 1898 by extracting the chemical compound from a uranium sample and distinguishing the brilliant green flame color of barium from the unknown compound's crimson color spectrum.
B) The discovery of eka-caesium in 1939 by examining the decay product energy levels in a sample of actinium-227/
C) The discovery of Gallium in 1871 spectroscopically by examining its unique violet spectrum in a sample of Sphalerite.
D) The discovery of Helium in 1868 by examining the wavelength of the elements burning in the chromosphere of the Sun.

Passage 3

The coffee plant, *Coffea*, is a flowering plant whose seeds, coffee beans, are used to brew the beverage coffee. Coffee beans are a major export for many developing countries, and thus the best conditions in which to grow the coffee plant have been rigorously studied. The best *Coffea* is generally grown in the "coffee belt" – the region around the globe which is within ten degrees latitude of the equator. There are many different species of the plant with slightly different optimal growing conditions. Below are the results of two studies on the best conditions for growing *Coffea arabica.*

Study I

Coffea arabica is planted in four fields at different elevations. The plants are left to mature for seven years, and then the beans are harvested. Yields of the harvests are recorded. Coffee is brewed using the same technique with beans from each of the four fields, and the resulting coffee is given a rating which ranges from Poor, to Fair, to Good, to Excellent by professional coffee "Master Tasters." Below are the results from this study:

Elevation above sea level	Bean Yield	Coffee Rating
500 m	120 kg	Fair
1000 m	350 kg	Excellent
1700 m	600 kg	Good
2200 m	400 kg	Poor

Study II

Different types of *Coffea arabica* have been found to produce different levels of caffeine in their beans. A corporation looking to produce a high-quality, low-caffeine strain of coffee commissioned a study to determine which factors result in low caffeine-producing beans. The firm conducting the study ran a comparison of different strains of *Coffea arabica* found across the globe. A table detailing this comparison is found below:

Strain	Elevation grown (altitude)	Latitude grown	Percent caffeine
1	500 m	10° N	4%
2	1200 m	4° S	5%
3	1200 m	0° (Equatorial)	5.5%
4	1700 m	8° S	4%
5	1700 m	5° N	6%

18. If the corporation which commissioned Study II makes a decision solely based on the results of this study, which coffee strain will they decide to produce?

A) 1
B) 1 and/or 3
C) 5
D) 4 and/or 1

19. If the corporation which commissioned Study II also incorporated data from Study I, which strain of *Coffea arabica* might they decide to grow?

A) 1
B) 2
C) 3
D) 4

20. Which of the following is a possible correlation between altitude at which *Coffea arabica* is grown and the resulting quality of the coffee brewed?

A) *Coffea arabica* grown at higher altitudes produces better coffee.
B) *Coffea arabica* grown at higher altitudes produces worse coffee.
C) The best coffee is produced by growing *Coffea arabica* at either very low or very high altitudes.
D) The best coffee is produced by growing *Coffea arabica* between altitudes of 1000-2000 m.

21. Which of the following is possibly correlated with caffeine content of a coffee bean?

A) The elevation at which the coffee plant was grown.
B) The latitude at which the coffee plant was grown.
C) The quality of the coffee brewed with the bean.
D) None of these are correlated with caffeine content.

22. A coffee producer is using the results of only Study I to determine the best location to grow coffee, and wants to maximize first yield and then quality. At which elevation should the coffee producer plant *Coffea arabica*?

A) 500 m
B) 1000 m
C) 1700 m
D) 2200 m

23. Which of the following may have been an untested variable which impacted the results of Study I?

A) The technique used to brew coffee with the beans of each of the four fields.
B) The quality of the soil in each of the four fields.
C) The elevation at which the plants were grown.
D) The species of coffee plant grown.

24. If a coffee producer wants to take all available data into account when deciding where best to grow coffee plants, which piece or pieces of data is needed to best link the results of these studies?

A) The strains of *Coffea arabica* grown in both Study I and Study II.
B) The bean yields of the strains grown in Study II.
C) The caffeine percentages of the coffee brewed in Study I.
D) The elevation, in feet, of the plants grown in both studies.

25. A third study done by the government of Costa Rica, a coffee-exporting nation, has found that higher caffeinated coffee is associated with *Coffea arabica* grown at latitudes closest to 0°. How could Study II be altered to verify or contradict this finding?

A) The different strains of *Coffea arabica* could be grown at different elevations along the equator.
B) The same strain of *Coffea arabica* could be grown at different elevations along the equator.
C) The same strain of *Coffea arabica* could be grown at the same elevations across different latitudes.
D) The different strains of *Coffea arabica* could be grown at different elevations and different latitudes.

26. Which of the following maps shows the areas, circled in red, where Study II was conducted?

A)

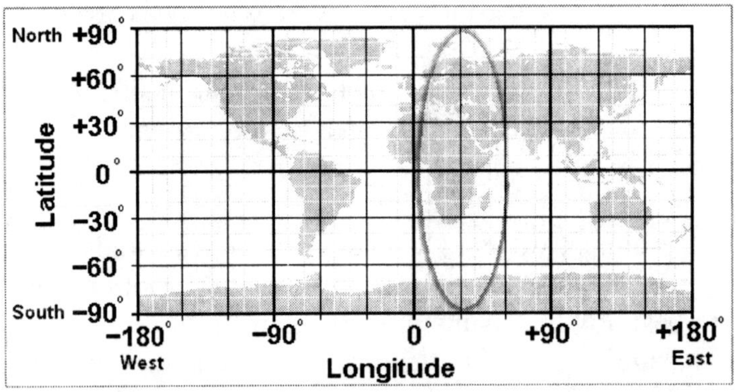

B)

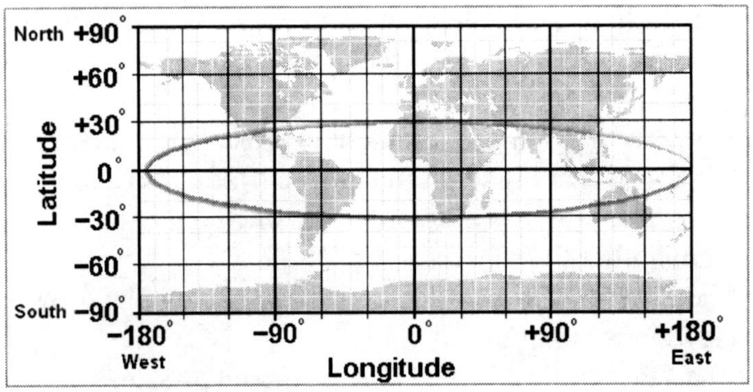

C)

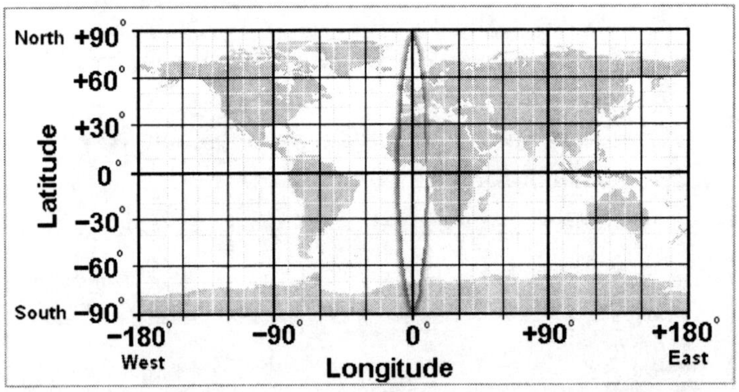

D)

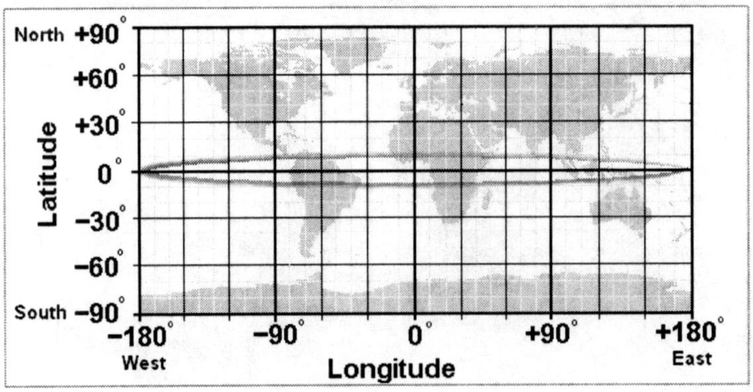

Passage 4

Blood types are used to describe agglutinogens, which are proteins attached to the surface of red blood cells. The genes which determine the agglutinogens a person's body will produce are inherited, and have three possible types: A, B, and O. An organism will produce antibodies, known as agglutinins, to guard against foreign agglutinogens. Below is a genotype showing the possible blood types arising from each possible combination of these genes. The resulting blood genotypes are shown in **bold**.

Blood Genotypes				
Inherited male blood type gene		Inherited female blood type gene		
		A	B	O
	A	**AA**	**AB**	**OA**
	B	**AB**	**BB**	**OB**
	O	**AO**	**BO**	**OO**

Phenotypes explain which genes in a given genotype are actually expressed as physical characteristics in an organism. For humans, the given blood types can produce four possible blood phenotypes: A, B, AB, and O. This is because the O blood gene is a recessive gene, and A and B blood type genes are co-dominant. Below is a chart showing blood phenotypes (in **bold**.)

Blood Phenotypes				
Inherited male blood type gene		Inherited female blood type gene		
		A	B	O
	A	**A**	**AB**	**A**
	B	**AB**	**B**	**B**
	O	**A**	**B**	**O**

27. If a child inherited a B blood type gene from his mother and a B blood type gene from his father, what will be his blood genotype?

A) AB
B) BB
C) B
D) BO

28. A person has blood type A. All of the following are possible blood genotypes for this person EXCEPT:

A) AA
B) AO
C) AB
D) OA

29. If a population has an equal distribution of each possible blood genotype, which will be the most common blood genotype in that population?

A) A
B) B
C) Types A and B will be equally common.
D) AB

30. If a person has blood phenotype B, which of the following is a possible combination of her inherited blood type genes?

A) An O from her mother and a B from her father.
B) A B from her mother and an A from her father.
C) An A from her mother and an A from her father.
D) An O from her mother and an A from her father.

31. Which of the following is the only combination of blood type genes that can result in a person having O type blood?

A) AO
B) OB
C) AB
D) OO

32. Two students take a blood typing test and find their blood types to be A and B, respectively. The students possibly share which of the following blood type genes?

A) A
B) B
C) O
D) It is not possible that they share any blood type genes.

33. In addition to the ABO blood type system, biologists have discovered the Rh system for typing blood as well. A common way of referring to this system is with "positive" or "negative;" for example saying that a person has AB- blood. This refers to the presence or absence of the *Rhesus factor*, a type of antigen, on the surface of the blood molecules. Including this factor in the ABO blood system, how many blood phenotypes are now possible?

A) 9
B) 15
C) 18
D) 81

34. Blood type is found in organisms other than humans. Apes have similar blood type systems to humans. Felines, however, do not carry the O type blood gene at all. Which of the following tables shows the possible blood genotypes for felines?

A)

Blood Genotypes in felines				
	Inherited female blood type gene			
Inherited male blood type gene		A	B	O
	A	**AA**	**AB**	**OA**
	B	**AB**	**BB**	**OB**
	O	**AO**	**BO**	**OO**

B)

Blood Genotypes in felines			
	Inherited female blood type gene		
Inherited male blood type gene		A	O
	A	**AA**	**OA**
	B	**AB**	**OB**
	O	**AO**	**OO**

C)

Blood Genotypes in felines			
	Inherited female blood type gene		
Inherited male blood type gene		A	B
	A	**AA**	**AB**
	B	**AB**	**BB**
	O	**AO**	**BO**

D)

Blood Genotypes in felines			
	Inherited female blood type gene		
Inherited male blood type gene		A	B
	A	**AA**	**AB**
	B	**AB**	**BB**

Passage 5

Formation of the Moon – conflicting theories

It is generally accepted among scientists who study the geology of the Moon, commonly known as selenologists, that the Moon was formed approximately 4.5 million years ago. Since the Apollo lunar missions of the late 1960s and 1970s, scientists have been gathering more data about the composition of the Moon, leading to several different theories about its formation. Below, two scientists present differing theories of the formation of the Moon.

Scientist 1: The lunar capture theory states that the Moon was formed elsewhere in the solar system and then captured by the gravitational pull of the Earth as it passed by. This makes sense given the composition of the Moon, which is 13% comprised of the iron oxide FeO. The Earth's mantle is 8% iron oxide, so it does not follow that the Moon is composed of the same material as the Earth. The gravitational conditions necessary to capture a body the size of the Moon are precise – it is much more likely that a body would collide with the Earth or pass by it, un-captured. This is not evidence that it could not have happened; that is why there is only one Moon.

Scientist 2: The giant impact theory holds that the Moon was formed when another planetary body, around the size of Mars, collided with the Earth 4.5 million years ago. The impact created a large amount of debris, which coalesced in orbit into the Moon. Estimates tested by computer simulations suggest that the debris could have formed the Moon within a month or within a century at the most. Oxygen isotopes found in rocks on the Moon by the Apollo missions match those found in rocks on Earth, suggesting that part of Earth went into the composition of the Moon. Other compounds found on the Moon in greater quantities than on Earth can be explained by the other body, which would also have contributed debris to the formation of the Moon.

35. Which of the following statements is most consistent with the lunar capture theory?

A) The Moon does not contain any material from the Earth in its composition.
B) The Moon is partially composed of material from another planetary body in the solar system which collided with the Earth.
C) Earth and the Moon have nearly identical levels of oxygen isotopes.
D) The Moon was probably formed around 4.5 million years ago.

36. Which of the following best describes what each scientist believes the Moon is made of?

A) Scientist 1: material from elsewhere in the solar system; Scientist 2: debris from Earth
B) Scientist 1: material from elsewhere in the solar system; Scientist 2: debris from Mars
C) Scientist 1: debris from the Earth and another planetary body; Scientist 2: material from elsewhere in the solar system
D) Scientist 1: material from elsewhere in the solar system; Scientist 2: debris from Earth and another planetary body

37. Which of the following discoveries would increase the support for Scientist 2's theory?

A) A planetary body in orbit around another planet in the solar system with the same mineral composition as the moon.
B) Oxygen isotopes found on the Moon similar to those found on Earth.
C) Material on Earth similar to the material on the Moon believed to be made from the other planetary body.
D) The occurrence of Jupiter capturing a small, Moon-like body.

38. The two scientists would likely agree with each of the following statements EXCEPT:

A) The Moon was formed 4.5 million years ago.
B) The probability of one planet "capturing" another body is very small.
C) The Moon is comprised of 13% iron oxide FeO.
D) The Moon could possibly have formed before the Earth.

39. Scientist 2 makes use of which tool of inquiry that Scientist 1 does not use?

A) Breakdowns of chemical compounds.
B) Computer modeling.
C) Gravitational physics.
D) Geological analysis of the moon's surface.

40. Assume that the lunar capture theory is correct. How could the evidence used by Scientist 2 best be interpreted to support this theory?

A) The Moon could have been formed during a time frame over a century, but elsewhere in the universe.
B) The Moon could have been formed out of some of the same material with which the Earth was formed, explaining their similar compositions.
C) The gravitational pull of the Earth could have been strong enough to influence the Moon as it passed by.
D) The Moon could have been captured by the Earth over 4.5 million years ago.

41. The giant impact theory is the one currently believed by most scientists. Which of the following is a weakness in this theory?

A) Rocks found on the Moon during the Apollo mission carried an isotopic signature identical to that of rocks on Earth.
B) Venus, another of the inner planets which is most similar to Earth, has a strong gravitational pull and is likely to have also been subjected to similar impacts. However, it does not have a moon.
C) The Earth's spin and the Moon's orbit are in identical directions, suggesting that the Moon spun off of the Earth after impact.
D) Similar collisions have been observed in other star systems and have resulted in the formation of debris disks, which orbit around stars and sometimes coalesce into a planetary body.

42. A scientist who studies the geology of the Moon is a:

A) Selenologist.
B) Lunologist.
C) Heliologist.
D) Astronomer.

Passage 6

There are two primary theories regarding adolescent cognitive development, the psychological development that occurs between puberty and the early twenties. This period of development is characterized by an emerging ability to think abstractly and to reason. These thinking processes are more complex than the concrete thinking evident in children. Adolescents begin to consider points of view other than their own, and to think about the process of thinking ("metacognition"). Two different theories of the process of cognitive development, which can be applied to adolescent cognitive development, are presented:

Constructivist perspective: This theory, developed by the Swiss psychologist and philosopher Jean Piaget, focuses on an individual's attempt to organize information about the world into structures. As an adolescent learns and assimilates more information, his or her cognitive (that is, thinking) structures advance in a way that allows the understanding of complex and abstract theories and ideas. The theory makes use of a block-stage structure, in which humans must first learn to understand certain types of information before they have the ability to understand more complex information. In this way, humans "construct" their own understanding of the world using tools that they had previously developed. Constructivist psychologists believe that learning occurs when a human encounters a fact, idea, or experience that contradicts what he or she already knows. The person then attempts to restore equilibrium and fit this new information into the knowledge structures he or she already has. This process is termed "equilibration." Practical knowledge and "real-world" experiences are critical in this process. Teachers function to guide students to new knowledge when they are ready to assimilate it into their existing structures for thinking.

Information-processing perspective: This theory, which is newer than the Constructivist perspective, derives from thinking of the mind as working similarly to how a computer processes. The brain processes symbols, which include ideas, facts, and all pieces of knowledge, in hierarchical schematics. Knowledge is organized along different paths: some knowledge is general, like knowing how to walk or gesture. Other knowledge is very specific, such as knowing how to sift flour. Knowledge can also be organized along the lines of how it is used: some knowledge is content knowledge, such as knowing the layout of roads in a city. Some knowledge is procedural, such as knowing how to drive a car. Humans learn by taking in new knowledge and creating a system for organizing it or fitting it into an existing organizational knowledge system. The purpose of teachers is to help students create effective systems for storing and remembering knowledge.

43. Metacognition is:

A) A theory regarding adolescent cognitive development.
B) The ability to understand complex information.
C) The way that a computer processes facts.
D) The process of thinking about thinking.

44. Both Constructivist and Information-processing perspectives seek to:

A) Explain the process of equilibration.
B) Explain adolescent psychology in particular.
C) Explain human processes for learning in general.
D) Undermine the other perspective.

45. Information-processing theory is explained in part by a comparison with:

A) Building blocks.
B) Computer systems.
C) Teaching.
D) Puberty.

46. A psychologist who subscribes to Information-processing theory would disagree with a Constructivist on which of the following points?

A) Adolescence is the time at which humans begin to think more abstractly.
B) New information can be integrated into one's existing understandings.
C) There exist different types of information.
D) Learning is largely a process of reordering systems of thinking, not of memorization.

47. A child is being observed by several psychologists. The child is given a set of complex and abstract information by a teacher. When asked questions about the information, the child's answers are nonsensical. Which theory does this explicitly support, and why?

A) Constructivist – the child must acquire more concrete information before she is able to understand complex information.
B) Constructivist - the complex information contradicts the information that the child already had.
C) Information-processing – the complex information is procedural information.
D) Information-processing – the teacher did not help the child to create an effective system for storing the complex information.

48. A teacher who is a proponent of the Information-processing theory of cognitive development may help his students to learn by doing which of the following?

A) Waiting until all of his students are ready to receive a new piece of information before giving it.
B) Telling students mnemonics, which are rhymes or acronyms used to help in memorizing information.
C) Have students work on complex projects.
D) Ensure that students always encounter information that contradicts what they already know.

49. A third perspective in cognitive development is Behaviorism, which holds that knowledge and behavior are enforced by patterns in the environment and by meaningful repetition of actions. Feedback from others is integral to the learning process, according to Behaviorists. Positive feedback reinforces desirable behaviors, which is how others learn. Constructivists and Behaviorists would agree on which of the following points?

A) Students who encounter new ideas are learning.
B) Practical, real-world experiences are necessary for learning.
C) Different types of knowledge must be learned in different ways.
D) Memorization and repetition are the most effective ways to process new information.

50. An Information-processing theorist would consider which of the following actions as demonstrating procedural knowledge?

A) Navigating a city.
B) Performing an operation.
C) Reciting the Pledge of Allegiance.
D) Discussing abstract ideas.

Passage 7

Biological taxonomists are those biologists who order our knowledge of species. Most students are familiar with the system of classifying organisms into kingdoms, phyla, classes, orders, families, genera, and species. Each of these classifications is more specific than the previous; for example, all known organisms are currently organized into six kingdoms. Within all of those kingdoms, all known organisms are organized into around 100 phyla. Species is the most specific classification, with only one known type of organism given each species name. There are hundreds of millions of species of known organisms.

Defining each of the classifications has been a difficulty within the field of biology ever since systems of classification first came into use during Ancient Greek times. The currently used modern system was structured by Carolus Linnaeus in 1734. Linnaeus, a Swedish botanist and zoologists, published *Systema Naturae*, which outlined the structure of a comprehensive system of taxonomy and which, with modifications, has been able to accommodate our growing understanding of living organisms.

On the following page is a tree showing a limited example of the taxonomy system.

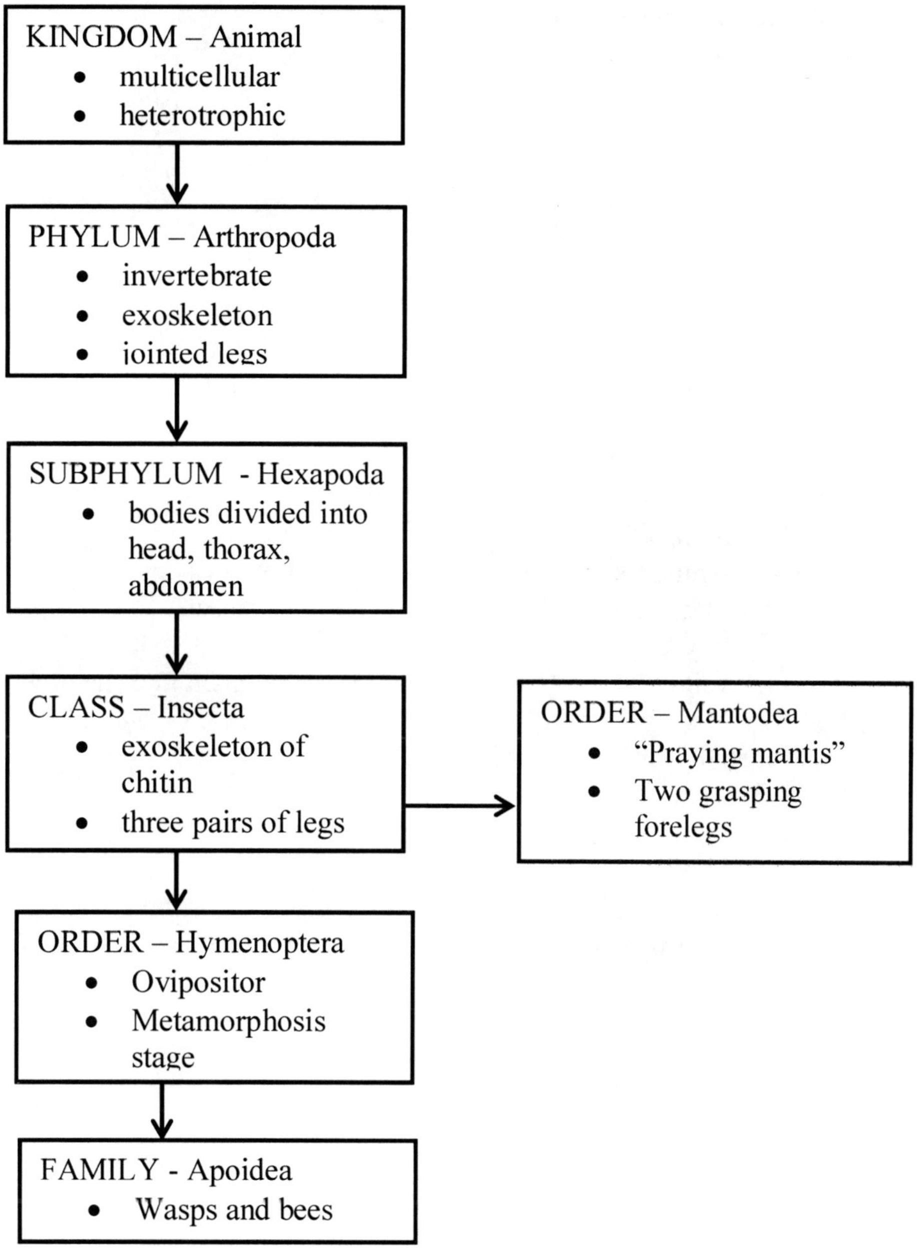
KINGDOM – Animal
multicellular
heterotrophic
PHYLUM – Arthropoda
invertebrate
exoskeleton
jointed legs
SUBPHYLUM - Hexapoda
bodies divided into head, thorax, abdomen
CLASS – Insecta
exoskeleton of chitin
three pairs of legs
ORDER – Mantodea
"Praying mantis"
Two grasping forelegs
ORDER – Hymenoptera
Ovipositor
Metamorphosis stage
FAMILY - Apoidea
Wasps and bees

51. The most general classification of living organisms is into:

A) Kingdoms.
B) Phyla.
C) Orders.
D) Genera.

52. Wasps and bees are in the phylum:

A) Arthropoda.
B) Hexapoda.
C) Hymenoptera.
D) Apoidea.

53. *Systema Naturae* by Carolus Linnaeus accomplished what?

A) Classifying all known living organisms.
B) Developing the kingdom classification categories.
C) Establishing the modern biological taxonomy system.
D) Exploring the taxonomical classification of insects.

54. Which of the following traits would classify an organism into the order Mantodea?

A) A metamorphosis phase in its life cycle.
B) A chitinous exoskeleton.
C) Grasping forelegs.
D) Compound eyes.

55. Which of the following organisms are most likely to be classified into the class Insecta?

A) Housefly
B) Tarantula
C) Earthworm
D) Scorpion

56. A group of scientists have discovered an organism in a rainforest that they believe has not been previously classified. The organism has a body divided into two sections. Which of the following cannot be true of the organism?

A) It has an exoskeleton.
B) It is closely related to the praying mantis.
C) It is in phylum Arthropoda.
D) It has a metamorphosis stage in its life cycle.

57. Organisms classified as Orthoptera generally have two pairs of wings and mouth parts formed for chewing. All Orthoptera are also Insecta. Within Orthoptera, there are several different types of families. Orthoptera is which of the following?

A) A phylum
B) A class
C) An order
D) A family

58. Given the information in the table, which of the following organisms would be impossible to classify at the order level?

A) An organism with three pairs of legs, an ovipositor, and predatory eating habits.
B) An organism with an exoskeleton of chitin, an ovipositor, and three pairs of legs.
C) An organism with a body divided into three sections, compound eyes, and two grasping forelegs.
D) An organism which is invertebrate, has an exoskeleton, and has heavy wings.

Science Section Question Bank – Answers

1. **C)** – The marks get farther apart as time goes on, because the magnet moves faster.
2. **C)** – Gravity is a constant which is working as long as the experiment is conducted on Earth. The others are possible sources of error in measurement or experimental set-up.
3. **C)**
4. **A)** – If the time intervals are larger, then the sparks will be farther apart – students will need to include more of the carbon paper in their records.
5. **B)**
6. **C)**
7. **A)**
8. **A)**
9. **B)** – An increase in gravity causes a decrease in acceleration, so the spark marks will be closer together.
10. **D)** – From the first paragraph of the passage.
11. **A)**
12. **D)** – This is not true.
13. **C)**
14. **D)**
15. **B)**
16. **A)**
17. **B)** – All the others give examples of using spectrum testing.
18. **D)**
19. **D)** – Strain 4 has a low caffeine percentage and is grown at a latitude associated with high yields and good quality.
20. **B)**
21. **D)**
22. **C)**
23. **B)** – All other variables are either explicitly tested or explicitly held constant.
24. **A)**
25. **C)** – All other variables must be held constant to test the effect of latitude on the percent of caffeine.
26. **D)** – The area between 10°N and 10°S of the equator is circled.
27. **B)** – Genotype shows both genes, not the expressed type.
28. **C)** – Also, genotype of AB would result in blood type AB, not A.
29. **C)**
30. **A)**
31. **D)**

32. C) – The students could have blood genotypes AO and BO.
33. C – There are 9 original phenotypes, and each can be positive or negative.
34. D)
35. A)
36. D)
37. C) – This would be evidence that the planetary body had indeed struck Earth.
38. D) – Only Scientist 1's theory is compatible with this statement.
39. B)
40. B)
41. B)
42. A)
43. D)
44. C)
45. B)
46. D)
47. A)
48. B)
49. B)
50. B)
51. A)
52. A)
53. C)
54. C)
55. A)
56. B) – This is the only one directly precluded by the organism not being in the class Insecta.
57. C)
58. A) – These characteristics fall into both orders illustrated on the table.

Chapter 9: Reading Section Question Bank

Directions:
On this test, you will have 35 minutes to read four passages and answer 40 questions (ten on each passage). Each set of ten questions appears directly after the relevant passage. You should select the answer choice that best answers the question. There is no time limit for work on the individual passages, so you can move freely between passages and refer to each as often as you'd like.

Passage 1
Prose - from "On Lying Awake at Night" by Stewart Edward White (public domain).

About once in so often you are due to lie awake at night. Why this is so I have never been able to discover. It apparently comes from no predisposing uneasiness of indigestion, no rashness in the matter of too much tea or tobacco, no excitation of unusual incident or stimulating conversation. In fact, you turn in with the expectation of rather a good night's rest. Almost at once the little noises of the forest grow larger, blend in the hollow bigness of the first drowse; your thoughts drift idly back and forth between reality and dream; when—*snap!*—you are broad awake!

For, unlike mere insomnia, lying awake at night in the woods is pleasant. The eager, nervous straining for sleep gives way to a delicious indifference. You do not care. Your mind is cradled in an exquisite poppy-suspension of judgment and of thought. Impressions slip vaguely into your consciousness and as vaguely out again. Sometimes they stand stark and naked for your inspection; sometimes they lose themselves in the mist of half-sleep. Always they lay soft velvet fingers on the drowsy imagination, so that in their caressing you feel the vaster spaces from which they have come. Peaceful-brooding your *faculties* receive. Hearing, sight, smell—all are preternaturally keen to whatever of sound and sight and woods perfume is abroad through the night; and yet at the same time active appreciation dozes, so these things lie on it sweet and cloying like fallen rose-leaves.

Nothing is more fantastically unreal to tell about, nothing more concretely real to experience, than this undernote of the quick water. And when you do lie awake at night, it is always making its unobtrusive appeal. Gradually its hypnotic spell works. The distant chimes ring louder and nearer as you cross the borderland of sleep. And then outside the tent some little woods noise snaps the thread. An owl hoots, a whippoorwill cries, a twig cracks beneath the cautious prowl of some night creature—at once the yellow sunlit French meadows puff away—you are staring at the blurred image of the moon spraying through the texture of your tent.

(You have cast from you with the warm blanket the drowsiness of dreams. A coolness, physical and spiritual, bathes you from head to foot. All your senses are keyed to the last vibrations. You hear the littler night prowlers; you glimpse the greater. A faint, searching woods perfume of dampness greets your nostrils. And somehow, mysteriously, in a manner not to be understood, the forces of the world seem in suspense, as though a touch might crystallize infinite possibilities into infinite power and motion. But the touch lacks. The forces hover on the edge of action, unheeding the little noises. In all humbleness and awe, you are a dweller of the Silent Places.

The night wind from the river, or from the open spaces of the wilds, chills you after a time. You begin to think of your blankets. In a few moments you roll yourself in their soft wool. Instantly it is morning.

And, strange to say, you have not to pay by going through the day unrefreshed. You may feel like turning in at eight instead of nine, and you may fall asleep with unusual promptitude, but your journey will begin clear-headedly, proceed springily, and end with much in reserve. No languor, no dull headache, no exhaustion, follows your experience. For this once your two hours of sleep have been as effective as nine.

1. In Paragraph 2, "*faculties*" is used to mean:
   A) Teachers.
   B) Senses.
   C) Imaginations.
   D) Capacities.

2. The author's opinion of insomnia is that:
   A) It is not a problem because nights without sleep are refreshing.
   B) It can happen more often when sleeping in the woods because of the noises in nature.
   C) It is generally unpleasant, but sometimes can be hypnotic.
   D) It is the best way to cultivate imagination.

3. By 'strange to say' in Paragraph 6, the author means:
   A) The experience of the night before had an unreal quality.
   B) The language used in describing the night before is not easily understood.
   C) It is not considered acceptable to express the opinion the author expresses.
   D) Contrary to expectations, one is well-rested after the night before.

4. How is this essay best characterized?
   A) A playful examination of a common medical problem.
   B) A curious look at both sides of an issue.
   C) A fanciful description of the author's experience.
   D) A horrific depiction of night hallucinations.

5. It can be reasonably inferred from this passage that the author regards nature in which of the following ways?

A) With fear.
B) With annoyance.
C) With appreciation.
D) With reverence.

6. Paragraph 2 describes a state of mind in which:

A) The mind is passively receiving impressions without examining them closely.
B) Great new ideas are forming.
C) Senses are heightened with great clarity.
D) Dreaming is deep and the outside world does not interfere.

7. Which of the following best describes the structure of this passage?

A) An essay in which the author describes an unpopular opinion and defends it with evidence.
B) An account given by the author of a personal experience which demonstrates a universal truth.
C) An essay which makes use of second-person narration to describe a vivid experience.
D) A detailed narration of a personal experience accompanied by an objective reaction to that experience.

8. In Paragraph 4 of this passage, "you:"

A) Are able to fall into sleep.
B) Become afraid of the noises in the woods.
C) Become more fully awake.
D) Are finally used to the "forces of the world."

9. The author of this piece is most likely:

A) A poet.
B) A psychologist.
C) A politician.
D) A natural biologist.

10. The author uses the phrase "preternaturally keen" in Paragraph 2 to tell the reader that "your" senses:

A) Are dozing.
B) Are heightened.
C) Are overwhelmed.
D) Are perceiving what is not real.

Passage 2

Natural Science - excerpted from Insects and Disease by Rennie W. Doane, a popular science account published in 1910 (public domain).

It has been estimated that there are about four thousand species or kinds of Protozoans, about twenty-five thousand species of Mollusks, about ten thousand species of birds, about three thousand five hundred species of mammals, and from two hundred thousand to one million species of insects, or from two to five times as many kinds of insects as all other animals combined.

Not only do the insects preponderate in number of species, but the number of individuals belonging to many of the species is absolutely beyond our comprehension. Try to count the number of little green aphis on a single infested rose-bush, or on a cabbage plant; guess at the number of mosquitoes issuing each day from a good breeding-pond; estimate the number of scale insects on a single square inch of a tree badly infested with San José scale; then try to think how many more bushes or trees or ponds may be breeding their millions just as these and you will only begin to comprehend the meaning of this statement.

As long as these myriads of insects keep, in what we are pleased to call their proper place, we care not for their numbers and think little of them except as some student points out some wonderful thing about their structure, life-history or adaptations. But since the dawn of history we find accounts to show that insects have not always kept to their proper sphere but have insisted at various times and in various ways in interfering with man's plans and wishes, and on account of their excessive numbers the results have often been most disastrous.

Insects cause an annual loss to the people of the United States of over $1,000,000,000. Grain fields are devastated; orchards and gardens are destroyed or seriously affected; forests are made waste places and in scores of other ways these little pests which do not keep in their proper places are exacting this tremendous tax from our people. These things have been known and recognized for centuries, and scores of volumes have been written about the insects and their ways and of methods of combating them.

Yellow fever, while not so widespread as malaria, is more fatal and therefore more terrorizing. Its presence and spread are due entirely to a single species of mosquito, *Stegomyia calopus*. While this species is usually restricted to tropical or semi-tropical regions it sometimes makes its appearance in places farther north, especially in summer time, where it may thrive for a time. The adult mosquito is black, conspicuously marked with white. The legs and abdomen are banded with white and on the thorax is a series of white lines which in well-preserved specimens distinctly resembles a lyre. These mosquitoes are essentially domestic insects, for they are very rarely found except in houses or in their immediate vicinity. Once they enter a room they will scarcely leave it except to lay their eggs in a near-by cistern, water-pot, or some other convenient place.

Their habit of biting in the daytime has gained for them the name of "day mosquitoes" to distinguish them from the night feeders. But they will bite at night as well as by day and many other species are not at all adverse to a daylight meal, if the opportunity offers, so this habit is not distinctive. The recognition of these facts has a distinct bearing in the methods adopted to prevent the spread of yellow fever. There are no striking characters or habits in the larval or pupal stages that would enable us to distinguish without careful examination this species from other similar forms with which it might be associated. For some time it was claimed that this species would breed only in clean water, but it has been found that it is not nearly so particular, some even claiming that it prefers foul water. I have seen them breeding in countless thousands in company with *Stegomyia scutellaris* and *Culex fatigans* in the sewer drains in Tahiti in the streets of Papeete. As the larva feed largely on bacteria one would expect to find them in exactly such places where the bacteria are of course abundant. The fact that they are able to live in any kind of water and in a very small amount of it well adapts them to their habits of living about dwellings.

11. In Paragraph 1, the author lists the amounts of different species of organisms in order to:

A) Illustrate the vast number of species in the world.
B) Demonstrate authority on the subject of insects.
C) Establish the relative importance of mollusks and birds.
D) Demonstrate the proportion of insects to other organisms.

12. What does the author mean by using "their proper place" at the beginning of paragraph 3?

A) The author is alluding to people's tendency to view insects as largely irrelevant to their lives.
B) The author feels that insects belong only outdoors.
C) The author wants the reader to feel superior to insects.
D) The author is warning that insects can evolve to affect the course of human events.

13. The main idea of this passage is best summarized as:

A) Disease-carrying mosquitoes have adapted to best live near human settlements.
B) Insects can have a detrimental effect on the economy by destroying crops.
C) Insects are numerous in both types of species and individuals within a species.
D) Although people do not always consider insects consequential, they can have substantial effects on human populations.

14. The use of "domestic" in Paragraph 5 most nearly means:

A) Originating in the United States.
B) Under the care of and bred by humans.
C) Fearful of the outdoors.
D) Living near human homes.

15. Which of the following ideas would best belong in this passage?

A) An historical example of the effect a yellow fever outbreak had on civilization.
B) A biological explanation of how diseases are transmitted from insects to humans.
C) A reference to the numbers of insects which live far away from human habitation.
D) Strategies for the prevention of yellow fever and malaria.

16. The passage indicates that mosquitos have all of the following patterns of behavior EXCEPT:

A) Biting humans during both the night and the day.
B) Traveling over moderate distances during the day to find sources of food.
C) Laying eggs near sources of bacteria.
D) Generally inhabiting tropical and semi-tropical regions.

17. Information in the final paragraph indicates that which of the following may be a method to reduce malaria deaths from mosquito bite transmission?

A) Staying indoors during nighttime.
B) Taking malarial preventative medications.
C) Limiting occurrences of standing water with bacteria on the surface.
D) Taking measures to eliminate the species *Stegomyia scutellaris* and *Culex fatigans* as well.

18. In non-tropical climates, *Stegomyia calopus* thrives in which season?

A) Winter
B) Spring
C) Summer
D) Fall

19. Which of the following best describes the structure of this passage?

A) A general discussion of the importance of insects to human populations which gives a specific example.

B) A discussion of two conflicting theories in biology which gives evidence for both.

C) A list of figures and statistics which, taken together, describe an epidemic.

D) An instructional manual for protecting human populations from *Stegomyia calopus.*

20. All of the following are used in this passage as examples of the impact insects can have on human populations EXCEPT:

A) Destruction of food sources.

B) Yellow fever epidemics.

C) Loss of profits.

D) Pollination of crops.

21. According to this passage, the number of insects on the planet is:

A) At least two times the number of all other organisms combined.

B) Beyond comprehension.

C) About one million.

D) Rising.

Passage 3

Social Sciences - (author Elissa Yeates):

The collapse of the arbitrage[1] firm Long-Term Capital Management (LTCM) in 1998 is explained by a host of different factors: its investments were based on a high level of leverage, for example, and it was significantly impacted by Russia's default on the ruble. However, sociologist Donald MacKenzie maintains that the main factor in LTCM's demise was that, like all arbitrage firms, it was subjected to the sociological phenomena of the arbitrage community; namely, imitation. Arbitrageurs, who are generally known to one another as members of a specific subset of the financial society, use decision-making strategies based not only on mathematical models or pure textbook reason, but also based upon their feelings and gut reactions toward the financial market and on the actions of their peers. This imitation strategy leads to the overlapping "superportfolio," which creates an inherent instability that leads to collapse, the most infamous example being LTCM.

The public opinion of the partners of the firm in 1998 was that it had acted cavalierly with borrowed capital. However, in actuality the firm's strategy was exceedingly

---

[1] "Arbitrage" is a financial strategy which takes advantage of the temporary price differences of a single asset in different markets.

conservative, with a diversified portfolio, overestimated risks, and carefully hedged investments. The firm even tested tactics for dealing with financial emergencies such as the collapse of the European Monetary Union. Before the 1998 crisis, those in LTCM were never accused of recklessness. Nor were they, as is sometimes explained, overly reliant on mathematical models. The statistical hubris explanation falters under MacKenzie's evidence that John Meriwether and the others who ran the firm made their investment decisions based more upon their intricate understandings of the arbitrage market rather than upon the pure results of mathematical analyses. The financial instability that was created was not the result of the decision-making of one firm; but rather, the collective patterns of decision-making of all of the arbitrage firms at the time.

The infamy of LTCM worked against the company. LTCM was composed of some of the most eminent minds in finance and it made devastating profits for the first few years that it was running. This led to imitation by other arbitrageurs who viewed the investments of LTCM as nearly sure bets. This type of replication of investment portfolios is not surprising, considering that arbitrageurs are all looking for similar types of pricing discrepancies and anomalies to exploit. The structure of arbitrageurs as a unique subset of the financial community who are largely personally known to one another further contributes to this phenomenon. Because of these factors over time the various players in the field of arbitrage created overlapping investments which MacKenzie dubs a "superportfolio." While LTCM alone may have created a geographically and industrially diverse portfolio, across the discipline of arbitrage as a whole capital flocked to similar investments.

Because of this superportfolio trend, multiple arbitrageurs were affected by the price changes of different assets caused by the actions of single independent firms. MacKenzie cites the example of the takeover of the investment bank Salomon Brothers by the Travelers Corporation. Salomon Brothers' portfolio, now under the management of someone who disliked the risks of arbitrage trading, liquidated its positions, which drove down the prices of assets in the markets in which it operated. The liquidation of the holdings of such a prominent player in the arbitrage game negatively affected the positions of every other firm that had a stake in those markets, including, of course, LTCM. This also illustrates the other sociological side of MacKenzie's argument: that arbitrageurs are subject to irrational internal pressures to cut their losses before their investments play out, which one of his interview subjects terms "queasiness" when faced with a stretch of losses.

22. The author includes the information presented in Paragraph 2 primarily to:

A) Explain that recklessness with borrowed capital is never profitable.
B) Explore the factors ultimately responsible for the demise of the arbitrage firm Long-Term Capital Management.
C) Laud the use of statistical models in calculating financial risks.
D) Present and dismiss several theories of the collapse of Long-Term Capital Management.

23. In Paragraph 3, "devastating" is used to mean:

A) Destructive
B) Attractive
C) Blasphemous
D) Considerable

24. Which of the following statements can be reasonably inferred from the passage?

A) Financial phenomena can be the result of human relationships rather than fluctuations in world markets.
B) Long-Term Capital Management would not have collapsed if its investors had been less audacious.
C) Arbitrageurs are known for acting independently from one another.
D) The public well understood the factors that led to the demise of Long-Term Capital Management in 1998.

25. The purpose of Paragraph 4 in this passage is to:

A) Refute the argument presented in the second paragraph of the passage.
B) Give a logical example of the phenomenon described in the introductory paragraph of the passage.
C) Give a step-by-step account of the demise of Long-Term Capital Management.
D) Argue that an understanding of sociology is crucial to successful financial practice.

26. Which of the following is a best description of the author's approach to the topic?

A) Curious exploration.
B) Gleeful detection.
C) Disgusted condemnation.
D) Serene indifference.

27. Which of the following most accurately summarizes the author's thesis?

A) If Long-Term Capital Management had developed a superportfolio, it would not have collapsed.
B) Financial markets are inherently instable because those who participate in them are subject to human faults.
C) Arbitrage firms should always endeavor to have geographically and industrially diverse investments.
D) Long-Term Capital Management collapsed because arbitrageurs across the industry were investing in the same things, which caused instability.

28. The word "hubris" in Paragraph 2 most nearly means:

A) Mathematical model.
B) Reliance.
C) Arrogance.
D) Denial.

29. Which of these facts would undermine the main argument of the passage?

A) The European Monetary Union was close to collapse in 1998.
B) Some arbitrage firms steered clear of the practice of superportfolios.
C) Arbitrageurs rarely communicate with one another or get information from the same source.
D) Mathematical models used in finance in the 1990s were highly reliable.

30. Which of the following would best support the argument made in Paragraph 3 of this passage?

A) An explanation of how other arbitrage firms were able to learn the tactics practiced by Long-Term Capital Management.
B) Examples of the differences between different investment portfolios of arbitrage firms.
C) An outline of sociological theories about decision-making processes.
D) A map showing the geographical diversity of arbitrage investors.

31. Which of the following questions is not explicitly addressed by the author in this passage?

A) What was the role investor risk-taking played in the collapse of the firm Long-Term Capital Management?
B) How do arbitrageurs interact with one another across the financial market?
C) What preventative steps could investors have taken to prevent being affected by the collapse of LTCM?
D) What tools do arbitrageurs tend to use in making their decisions?

32. According to the author, all of the following are tendencies of those who practice arbitrage EXCEPT:

A) To cut losses before a situation has played out.
B) To consult mathematical models.
C) To act on information revealed by others.
D) To look for investments that others are not seeking.

33. In Paragraph 3, "infamy" is used to mean:

A) Fame
B) Honor
C) Disrepute
D) Notoriety

Passage 4

Prose – This passage is excerpted from Robert Louis Stevenson's classic novel *Treasure Island* *(public domain). In this passage, the narrator tells about an old sailor staying at his family's inn.*

He had taken me aside one day and promised me a silver fourpenny on the first of every month if I would only keep my "weather-eye open for a seafaring man with one leg" and let him know the moment he appeared. Often enough when the first of the month came round and I applied to him for my wage, he would only blow through his nose at me and stare me down, but before the week was out he was sure to think better of it, bring me my four-penny piece, and repeat his orders to look out for "the seafaring man with one leg."

How that personage haunted my dreams, I need scarcely tell you. On stormy nights, when the wind shook the four corners of the house and the surf roared along the cove and up the cliffs, I would see him in a thousand forms, and with a thousand diabolical expressions. Now the leg would be cut off at the knee, now at the hip; now he was a monstrous kind of a creature who had never had but the one leg, and that in the middle of his body. To see him leap and run and pursue me over hedge and ditch was the worst of nightmares. And altogether I paid pretty dear for my monthly fourpenny piece, in the shape of these abominable fancies.

But though I was so terrified by the idea of the seafaring man with one leg, I was far less afraid of the captain himself than anybody else who knew him. There were nights when he took a deal more rum and water than his head would carry; and then he would sometimes sit and sing his wicked, old, wild sea-songs, minding nobody; but sometimes he would call for glasses round and force all the trembling company to listen to his stories or bear a chorus to his singing. Often I have heard the house shaking with "Yo-ho-ho, and a bottle of rum," all the neighbors joining in for dear life, with the fear of death upon them, and each singing louder than the other to avoid remark. For in these fits he was the most overriding companion ever known; he would slap his hand on the table for silence all round; he would fly up in a passion of anger at a question, or sometimes because none was put, and so he judged the company was not following his story. Nor would he allow anyone to leave the inn till he had drunk himself sleepy and reeled off to bed.

His stories were what frightened people worst of all. Dreadful stories they were—about hanging, and walking the plank, and storms at sea, and the Dry Tortugas, and wild deeds and places on the Spanish Main. By his own account he must have lived his life among some of the wickedest men that God ever allowed upon the sea, and the language in which he told these stories shocked our plain country people almost as much as the crimes that he described. My father was always saying the inn would be ruined, for people would soon cease coming there to be tyrannized over and put down, and sent shivering to their beds; but I really believe his presence did us good. People were frightened at the time, but on looking back they rather liked it; it was a fine excitement in a quiet country life, and there was even a party of the younger men who pretended to admire him, calling him a "true sea-dog" and a "real old salt" and such like names, and saying there was the sort of man that made England terrible at sea.

In one way, indeed, he bade fair to ruin us, for he kept on staying week after week, and at last month after month, so that all the money had been long exhausted, and still my father never plucked up the heart to insist on having more. If ever he mentioned it, the captain blew through his nose so loudly that you might say he roared, and stared my poor father out of the room. I have seen him wringing his hands after such a rebuff, and I am sure the annoyance and the terror he lived in must have greatly hastened his early and unhappy death.

34. What does the phrase "that personage" reference at the beginning of Paragraph 2?

A) The old sailor staying at the inn.
B) The narrator's father.
C) The seafaring man with one leg.
D) A sailor from the Spanish Main.

35. The author's inclusion of anecdotes in Paragraph 3 is to:

A) Illustrate how others view the captain.
B) Explain the narrator's relationship with the captain.
C) Give more background information about the inn where the narrator lives.
D) Recount old seafaring lore.

36. What emotion does the author intend to evoke in the reader with the first sentence in Paragraph 2, "How that personage haunted…"?

A) Dreaminess
B) Familiarity
C) Amusement
D) Horror

37. Which paragraph serves to evoke the life lived by sailors at sea?

A) 1
B) 2
C) 3
D) 4

38. "Diabolical" in Paragraph 2 most nearly means:

A) Fiendish.
B) Enraged.
C) Judgmental.
D) Contorted.

39. What kind of character does the author reveal the captain to be in Paragraph 3?

A) Temperamental
B) Generous
C) Jocund
D) Reserved

40. What does the author reveal about the narrator in Paragraph 5?

A) The narrator is afraid of the captain.
B) The narrator is eager to go to sea.
C) The narrator grew up in poverty.
D) The narrator lost his father at an early age.

41. What does the narrator wish to convey by saying, "I paid pretty dear for my monthly fourpenny piece" at the end of Paragraph 2?

A) He had to give the captain a valuable coin each month to preserve his safety.
B) He earned the fourpenny by keeping a watch for the man with one leg, which gave him terrible nightmares.
C) He had to pay with a fourpenny coin each month to stay at this inn.
D) By accepting the captain's fourpenny piece, the narrator created a problematic friendship with him.

42. "Tyrannized" in Paragraph 4 is used to most nearly mean:

A) Bullied.
B) Frightened.
C) Robbed.
D) Ejected.

43. Which of the following statements about this passage is false?

A) It is unclear whether the "seafaring man with one leg" actually exists.
B) The narrator harbors a serious grudge against the captain.
C) The narrator is interested in the captain's stories.
D) Most people who populate the story are afraid of the captain.

44. The phrase "in a thousand forms, and with a thousand diabolical expressions" is an example of which literary device?

A) Hyperbole
B) Metaphor
C) Foreshadowing
D) Symbolism

45. The captain lists as examples all of the following hazards of the sea EXCEPT:

A) Hangings
B) Wicked men
C) Walking the plank
D) Sea monsters

46. Which of the following can be reasonably inferred from the narrative?

A) Singing was frowned upon in the community.
B) The narrator never knew his mother.
C) The captain is afraid of the seafaring man with one leg.
D) The narrator went on to become a pirate.

47. By "they rather liked it" at the end of Paragraph 4, the author is trying to convey that:

A) The patrons of the inn enjoyed singing.
B) The captain and other appreciated the rum available for sale at the inn.
C) The narrator and his friends found the stories the captain told thrilling.
D) The captain provided entertainment at the inn, which would otherwise be boring.

Passage 5

Humanities - The following passage is excerpted from A History of Art for Beginners and Students by Clara Erskine Clement, first published in 1887 (public domain).

Egyptian painting is principally found on the walls of temples and tombs, upon columns and cornices, and on small articles found in burial places. There is no doubt that it was used as a decoration; but it was also intended to be useful, and was so employed as to tell the history of the country;—its wars, with their conquests and triumphs, and the lives of the kings, and many other stories, are just as distinctly told by pictures as by the hieroglyphics or Egyptian writings. We can scarcely say that Egyptian painting is beautiful; but it certainly is very interesting.

The Egyptians had three kinds of painting: one on flat surfaces, a second on bas-reliefs, or designs a little raised and then colored, and a third on designs in *intaglio*, or hollowed out from the flat surface and the colors applied to the figures thus cut out. They had no knowledge of what we call perspective, that is, the art of representing a variety of objects on one flat surface, and making them appear to be at different distances from us—their drawing and their manner of expressing the meaning of what they painted were very crude. As far as the pictorial effect is concerned, there is very little difference between the three modes of Egyptian painting; their general appearance is very nearly the same.

The Egyptian artist sacrificed everything to the one consideration of telling his story clearly; the way in which he did this was sometimes very amusing, such as the making one man twice as tall as another in order to signify that he was of high position, such as a king or an officer of high rank. When figures are represented as following each other, those that are behind are frequently taller than those in front, and sometimes those that are farthest back are ranged in rows, with the feet of one row entirely above the heads of the others. An illustration of the storming of a fort by a king and his sons shows this. The sons are intended to be represented as following the father, and are in a row, one above the other.

For the representation of water, a strip of blue filled in with perpendicular zigzag black lines was used. From these few facts you can understand how unformed and awkward Egyptian pictures seem if we compare them with the existing idea of what is beautiful. There appear to have been certain fixed rules for the use of colors, and certain objects were always painted in the colors prescribed for them. The background of a picture was always of a single, solid color; Egyptian men were painted in a reddish brown, and horses were of the same shade; and women were generally yellow, sometimes a lighter brown than the men. The draperies about the figures were painted in pleasing colors, and were sometimes transparent, so that the figures could be seen through them.

The execution of Egyptian paintings was very mechanical. One set of workmen prepared the plaster on the wall for the reception of the colors; another set drew all the outlines in red; then, if chiseling was to be done, another class performed this labor; and, finally, still others put on the colors. Of course nothing could be more matter-of-fact than such painting as this, and under such rules an artist of the most lofty genius and imagination would find it impossible to express his conceptions in his work. We know all this because some of these pictures exist in an unfinished condition, and are left in the various stages of execution; then, too, there are other pictures of the painters at their work, and all these different processes are shown in them. The outline drawing is the best part of Egyptian painting, and this is frequently very cleverly done.

As I have intimated, the greatest value of Egyptian painting is that it gives us a clear record of the habits and customs of a very ancient people—of a civilization which has long since passed away, and of which we should have a comparatively vague and unsatisfactory notion but for this picture-history of it. The religion, the political history, and the domestic life of the ancient Egyptians are all placed before us in these paintings. Through a study of them we know just how they hunted and fished, gathered their fruits, tilled the soil, and cooked the food, played games, danced, and practiced gymnastics, conducted their scenes of festivity and mourning—in short, how they lived under all circumstances. Thus you see that Egyptian painting is a very important example of the way in which pictures can teach us; you will also notice that it is not even necessary that they should be pretty in order that we may learn from them.

One cannot study Egyptian painting without feeling sorry for the painters; for in all the enormous amount of work done by them no one man was recognized—no one is now remembered. We know some of the names of great Egyptian architects which are written in the historical rolls; but no painter's name has been thus preserved. The fact that no greater progress was made is a proof of the discouraging influences that must have been around these artists, for it is not possible that none of them had imagination or originality: there must have been some whose souls were filled with poetic visions, for some of the Egyptian writings show that poetry existed in ancient Egypt. But of what use could imagination be to artists who were governed by the laws of a narrow priesthood, and hedged about by a superstitious religion which even laid down rules for art?

For these reasons we know something of Egyptian art and nothing of Egyptian artists, and from all these influences it follows that Egyptian painting is little more than an illuminated alphabet or a child's picture-history. In the hieroglyphics, or writing characters of Egypt, it often occurs that small pictures of certain animals or other objects stand for whole words, and it appears that this idea was carried into Egyptian painting, which by this means became simply a picture chronicle, and never reached a point where it could be called truly artistic or a high art.

48. According to the author, all of the following are kinds of ancient Egyptian paintings EXCEPT:

A) Paintings on flat surfaces.
B) Designs in *intaglio.*
C) Paintings on curved pottery.
D) Designs in bas-relief.

49. The author would agree that ancient Egyptian art:

A) Is of little value to art historians.
B) Proves that ancient Egyptians had no imagination.
C) Is comprised of a wide variety of styles.
D) Illuminates daily life in ancient Egypt.

50. The details shared in Paragraph 4 serve to support which of the author's opinions?

A) The general appearance of all ancient Egyptian paintings is nearly the same.
B) Egyptian painting is very interesting.
C) The artists in ancient Egypt sacrificed everything to tell a story.
D) One feels sorry for ancient Egyptian painters.

51. The existence of ancient Egyptian paintings in an unfinished condition teaches us:

A) That the artists were subject to religious laws.
B) The process by which these paintings were made.
C) That different classes of laborers performed each step of the painting process.
D) That the artists had no understanding of visual perspective.

52. The author describes the illustration of the storming of the fort in order to prove which of her points?

A) There are three types of ancient Egyptian paintings.
B) Ancient Egyptian artists used unrealistic imagery to demonstrate objects at different distances.
C) The way in which ancient Egyptian paintings were made was very mechanical.
D) Ancient Egyptian art is not considered beautiful by modern standards.

53. At the beginning of Paragraph 6, the word "intimated" most nearly means:

A) Bragged.
B) Argued.
C) Mentioned.
D) Whispered.

54. All of the following aspects of ancient Egyptian life can be understood by studying paintings EXCEPT:

A) How they mourned the dead.
B) The history of their politics.
C) How their paintings were made.
D) Who their artists were.

55. Which of the following artifacts, if found, would challenge the author's arguments?

A) A papyrus scroll depicting a team of ancient Egyptians working on a single painting.
B) A painting which made use of both *intaglio* and bas-relief designs.
C) An Egyptian painting demonstrating abstract concepts.
D) A set of tools which were used to carve bas-relief designs into plaster.

56. In Paragraph 2, the word "crude" in the next to last sentence most nearly means:

A) Not sophisticated.
B) Offensive.
C) Not well-preserved.
D) Not varied.

57. Which of the following questions is NOT addressed in this passage?

A) What are hieroglyphics?
B) What were the stages in creating art in ancient Egypt?
C) Did poetry exist in ancient Egypt?
D) Why did ancient Egyptian artists not use perspective?

58. From the passage, one can reasonably infer that:

A) Ancient Egyptian civilizations lasted for hundreds of years.
B) Art historians work frequently with archeologists.
C) No ancient civilizations made use of perspective in their art.
D) Ancient Egyptians were familiar with horses.

59. One of the points made in Paragraph 7 is that:

A) Religious art can be creative.
B) Artists who are not allowed to express themselves are to be pitied.
C) The ancient Egyptian society did not progress.
D) Ancient Egyptian art is valuable for what it teaches us.

60. Which of the following is the author mostly likely to consider "high art"?

A) A drawing which accurately depicts an aspect of daily life.
B) A reimagining of a landscape done abstractly.
C) A beautiful carving of a building in proportion.
D) A religious scene done in *intaglio.*

Reading Section Question Bank – Answers

1. B)
2. C)
3. D)
4. C)
5. C)
6. A)
7. C)
8. C)
9. A)
10. D)
11. D)
12. A)
13. D)
14. D)
15. A)
16. B)
17. C)
18. C)
19. A)
20. D)
21. B)
22. D)
23. D)
24. A)
25. B)
26. A)
27. D)
28. C)
29. C)
30. A)
31. C)
32. D)
33. D)
34. C)
35. A)
36. D)
37. D)
38. A)
39. A)
40. D)
41. B)
42. A)
43. B)
44. A)
45. D)
46. C)
47. D)
48. C)
49. D)
50. A)
51. B)
52. B)
53. C)
54. D)
55. C)
56. A)
57. D)
58. D)
59. B)
60. B)

Chapter 10: Math Section Question Bank

Section 1: Percent/Part/Whole, Percent Change, Repeated Percent Change, Simple Interest

1. In a class of 42 students, 18 are boys. Two girls get transferred to another school. What percent of students remaining are girls?
A) 14%
B) 16%
C) 52.4%
D) 60%
E) None of the above

2. A payroll check is issued for $500.00. If 20% goes to bills, 30% of the remainder goes to pay entertainment expenses, and 10% of what is left is placed in a retirement account, then approximately how much is remaining?
A) $150
B) $250
C) $170
D) $350
E) $180

3. A painting by Van Gogh increased in value by 80% from year 1995 to year 2000. If in year 2000, the painting is worth $7200, what was its value in 1995?
A) $1500
B) $2500
C) $3000
D) $4000
E) $5000

4. "Dresses and Ties" sells a particular dress for $60 dollars. But, they decide to discount the price of that dress by 25%. How much does the dress cost now?
A) $55
B) $43
C) $45
D) $48
E) $65

5. A sweater goes on sale for 30% off. If the original price of the sweater was $70, what is the discounted price?
A) $48
B) $49
C) $51
D) $65
E) $52

6. If the value of a car depreciates by 60% over ten years, and its value in the year 2000 is $2500, what was its value in the year 1990?
A) $6000
B) $6230
C) $6250
D) $6500
E) $6600

7. If an account is opened with a starting balance of $500, what is the amount in the account after 3 years if the account pays compound interest of 5%?
A) $560.80
B) $578.81
C) $564.50
D) $655.10
E) $660.00

8. A piece of memorabilia depreciates by 1% every year. If the value of the memorabilia is $75000, what will it be 2 years from now? Give the answer as a whole number.
A) $74149
B) $74150
C) $73151
D) $71662
E) $73507

9. A dress is marked down by 20% in an effort to boost sales for one week. After that week, the price of the dress is brought back to the original value. What percent did the price of the dress have to be increased from its discounted price?
A) 20%
B) 25%
C) 120%
D) 125%
E) 15%

10. A car dealer increases the price of a car by 30%, but then discounts it by 30%. What is the relationship between the final price and the original price?
A) .91x : x
B) .98x : x
C) 1:1
D) .88x : x
E) .75x : x

Math Section Question Bank: Section 1 – Answers

#1 Solution
Answer: E) None of the above.
The entire class has 42 students, of which 18 are boys, meaning 42-18 = 24 is the number of girls. Out of these 24 girls, 2 leave, so 22 girls are left. The total number of students is now 42-2 = 40.
22/40 * 100 = 55%
Reminder: If you forget to subtract 2 from the total number of students, you will end up with 60% as the answer. Sometimes you may calculate an answer that has been given as a choice; it can still be incorrect. Always check your answer.
Skill: Percent/Part/Whole

#2 Solution
Answer: B)
If out of the entire paycheck, 20% is first taken out, then the remainder is 80%. Of this remainder, if 30% is used for entertainment, then (.8-.80*.30) = .560 is left. If 10% is put into a retirement account, then (.56- .56*.1) = .504 is remaining. So out of $500, the part that remains is 50%, which is $252.
Skill: Percent/Part/Whole

#3 Solution
Answer: D)
In 2005, the value was 1.8 times its value in 1995. So 1.8x = 7200 → x = 4000.
Skill: Percent/Part/Whole

#4 Solution
Answer: C)
60 * (100-25)/100 → 60*.75 = 45.
Skill: Percent Change

#5 Solution
Answer: B)
New price = original price * (1 – discount) → new price = 70(1-.3) = 49.
Skill: Percent Change

#6 Solution
Answer: C)
$Value_{2000}$ = Original price * (1-.6) → 2500 = .4P = 2500 → P = 6250.
Skill: Percent Change

#7 Solution
Answer: B)
Amount = $P(1 + r)^t = 500*1.05^3$ = $578.81.
Skill: Compound Interest

#8 Solution

Answer: E)

Final value = $75000(1 - .1)^2 = 73507$.

Skill: Repeated Percent Change

#9 Solution

Answer: B)

If the original price of the dress was x, then the discounted price would be 0.8x. To increase the price from .8x to x, the percent increase would be (x - .8x)/.8x * 100 = 25%.

Skill: Percent/Part/Whole

10 Solution

Answer: A)

Let the original price of the car be x. After the 30% increase, the price is 1.3x. After discounting the increased price by 30%, it now is .7 * 1.3x = .91x. Therefore, the ratio of the final price to the original price = .91x : x.

Skill: Percentage and Ratio

Section 2: Mean, Median, Mode, Combined Averages

1. If test A is taken 5 times with an average result of 21, and test B is taken 13 times with an average result of 23, what is the combined average?
   A) 22.24
   B) 22.22
   C) 22.00
   D) 22.44
   E) 24.22

2. A set of data has 12 entries. The average of the first 6 entries is 12, the average of the next two entries is 20, and the average of the remaining entries is 4. What is the average of the entire data set?
   A) 10
   B) 10.67
   C) 11
   D) 12.67
   E) 10.5

3. What is the average score of 8 tests where the score for 3 tests is 55, the score for two tests is 35, and the remaining tests have scores of 70?
   A) 50.3
   B) 52.5
   C) 55.1
   D) 56.0
   E) 55.6

4. The temperatures over a week are recorded as follows:

Day	High	Low
Monday	80	45
Tuesday	95	34
Wednesday	78	47
Thursday	79	55
Friday	94	35
Saturday	67	46
Sunday	76	54

   What is the approximate average high temperature and average low temperature during the week?
   A) 90, 50
   B) 80, 40
   C) 81, 45
   D) 82, 46
   E) 81, 47

5. Twelve teams competed in a mathematics test. The scores recorded for each team are: 29, 30, 28, 27, 35, 43, 45, 50, 46, 37, 44, and 41. What is the median score?
A) 37
B) 41
C) 39
D) 44
E) 45

6. A class of 10 students scores 90, 78, 45, 98, 84, 79, 66, 87, 78, and 94. What is the mean score? What is the median score? What is the mode?
A) 69.9, 81.5, 78
B) 79.9, 80, 78
C) 79.9, 87, 76
D) Not enough information given.
E) None of the above.

7. A shop sells 3 kinds of t-shirts: one design sells for \$4.50, the second for \$13.25, and the third for \$15.50. If the shop sold 8 shirts of the first design, 12 shirts of the second design, and 4 shirts of the third design, what was the average selling price of the shirts?
A) \$10.71
B) \$10.25
C) \$14.55
D) \$12.55
E) \$5.80

Math Section Question Bank: Section 2 – Answers

#1 Solution
Answer: D)
If test A avg = 21 for 5 tests, then sum of test A results = 21 * 5 = 105.
If test B avg = 23 for 13 tests, then sum of test B results = 23 * 13 = 299.
So total result = 299 + 105 = 404.
Average of all tests = 404/(5 + 13) = 404/18 = 22.44.
Skill: Combined Averages

#2 Solution
Answer: B)
The average of the first 6 points is 12 → $s_1/6 = 12$ → $s_1 = 72$; s_1 is the sum of the first 6 points.
The average of the next 2 points is 20 → $s_2/2 = 20$ → $s_2 = 40$; s_2 is the sum of the next 2 points.
The average of the remaining 4 points is 4 → $s_3/4 = 4$ → $s_3 = 16$; s_3 is the sum of the last 4 points.
The sum of all the data points = 72+40+16 = 128.
The average = 128/12 = 10.67.
Skill: Mean, Median, Mode

#3 Solution
Answer: E)
Average = (3 * 55 + 2 * 35 + 3 * 70)/8→Average = 55.625.
Skill: Combined Averages

#4 Solution
Answer: C)
Average of high s= (80 + 95 + 78 + 79 + 94 + 67 + 76)/7 = 81.29.
Average of low s= (45 + 34 + 47 + 55 + 35 + 46 + 54)/7 = 45.14.
Skill: Mean, Median, Mode

#5 Solution
Answer: C)
To find the median, we first have to put the list in order:
27, 28, 29, 30, 35, 37, 41, 43, 44, 45, 46, 50.
The middle two scores are 37 and 41, and their average is 39.
Skill: Mean, Median, Mode

#6 Solution

Answer: E) None of the above

The mean is just the total score/number of scores → 90 +....+ 94)/10 → 79.9.
The median is the score located in the middle. The middle of the set of the numbers is between 84 and 79. The average of these two scores is 81.5.
The mode is the number that occurs the most: 78.
Skill: Mean, Median, Mode

#7 Solution

Answer: A)

Multiply each t-shirt price with the number sold; add them together and divide by the total number of shirts sold.
So Average Price = (4.50 * 8 + 13.25 * 12 + 15.50 * 4)/(8 + 12 + 4) → $10.71.
Skill: Combined Averages

Section 3: Exponents & Roots

1. What is $x^2y^3z^5/y^2z^{-9}$?
A) y^5z^4
B) yz^4
C) x^2yz^{14}
D) $x^2y^5z^4$
E) xyz

2. What is k if $(2m^3)^5 = 32m^{k+1}$?
A) 11
B) 12
C) 13
D) 14
E) 15

3. What is $x^5y^4z^3/x^{-3}y^2z^{-4}$?
A) $x^6y^4z^7$
B) x^8yz^7
C) x^6yz^7
D) $x^8y^2z^7$
E) $x^6y^2z^7$

4. Evaluate $(a^2*a^{54}+a^{56}+(a^{58}/a^2))/a^4$.
A) a^{56}
B) $3a^{56}$
C) $3a^{52}$
D) $3a^{54}$
E) a^{54}

5. $9^m = 3^{-1/n}$. What is mn?
A) .5
B) 2
C) -2
D) -.5
E) -1

6. If $2^a*4^a = 32$, what is a?
A) 1/3
B) 2/3
C) 1
D) 4/3
E) 5/3

7. Evaluate $\sqrt{3} + 2\sqrt{3} * \sqrt{3} + (\sqrt{3})^2 + \sqrt[4]{256}$

A) 16
B) 13
C) $\sqrt{3} + \sqrt{13}$
D) 4
E) $13 + \sqrt{3}$

Math Section Question Bank: Section 3 – Answers

#1 Solution
Answer: C)
$x^2y^3z^5/y^2z^{-9} = x^2y^3z^5 * y^{-2}z^9$ which gives the answer $x^2y^{(3-2)}z^{(5+9)} \rightarrow x^2yz^{14}$.
Skill: Exponents

#2 Solution
Answer: D)
Expand $(2m^3)^5$ to give $32m^{15}$. So$32m^{15} = 32m^{k+1} \rightarrow k+1 = 15 \rightarrow k = 14$.
Skill: Exponents

#3 Solution
Answer: D)
$x^5y^4z^3/x^{-3}y^2z^{-4} = x^5y^4z^3 * x^3y^{-2}z^4 = x^8y^2z^7$
Skill: Exponents

#4 Solution
Answer: C)
$(a^2*a^{54}+a^{56}+ (a^{58}/a^2))/a^4 = (a^{54}+2+a^{56}+a^{58}-2)a^{-4} = 3a^{56}-4 = 3a^{52}$.
Skill: Exponents

#5 Solution
Answer: D)
$9^m$is the same as 3^{2m}.
So $3^{2m} = 3^{-1/n} \rightarrow 2m = -1/n \rightarrow mn = -.5$.
Skill: Exponents

#6 Solution
Answer: E)
$2^a * 4^a$ can be re-written as $2^a * (2^2)^a$.
$32 = 2^5$.
Therefore, $2^{(a+2a)} = 2^5 \rightarrow 3a = 5 \rightarrow a = 5/3$.
Skill: Exponents

#7 Solution
Answer: E)
This evaluates to $\sqrt{3} + 6 + 3 + 4$, or $13+\sqrt{3}$.
Skill: Roots

Section 4: Algebraic Equations

1. The number 568cd should be divisible by 2, 5, and 7. What are the values of the digits c and d?
   A) 56835
   B) 56830
   C) 56860
   D) 56840
   E) 56800

2. Carla is 3 times older than her sister Megan. Eight years ago, Carla was 18 years older than her sister. What is Megan's age?
   A) 10
   B) 8
   C) 9
   D) 6
   E) 5

3. What is the value of $f(x) = (x^2-25)/(x+5)$ when $x = 0$?
   A) -1
   B) -2
   C) -3
   D) -4
   E) -5

4. Four years from now, John will be twice as old as Sally will be. If Sally was 10 eight years ago, how old is John?
   A) 35
   B) 40
   C) 45
   D) 50
   E) 55

5. I have some marbles. I give 25% to Vic, 20% to Robbie, 10% to Jules. I then give 6/20 of the remaining amount to my brother, and keep the rest for myself. If I end up with 315 marbles, how many did I have to begin with?
   A) 1000
   B) 1500
   C) 3500
   D) 400
   E) 500

6. I have some marbles. I give 25% to Vic, 20% of the remainder to Robbie, 10% of that remainder to Jules and myself I then give 6/20 of the remaining amount to my brother, and keep the rest for myself. If I end up with 315 marbles, how many did I have to begin with?
   A) 800
   B) 833
   C) 834
   D) 378
   E) 500

7. If $x = 5y + 4$, what is the value of y if $x = 29$?
   A) 33/5
   B) 5.5
   C) 5
   D) 0
   E) 29/5

8. A bag of marbles has 8 marbles. If I buy 2 bags of marbles, how many more bags of marbles would I need to buy to have a total of at least 45 marbles?
   A) 3
   B) 4
   C) 5
   D) 6
   E) 29

9. A factory that produces widgets wants to sell them each for $550. It costs $50 for the raw materials for each widget, and the startup cost for the factory was $10000. How many widgets have to be sold so that the factory can break even?
   A) 10
   B) 20
   C) 30
   D) 40
   E) 50

10. Expand $(3x - 4)(6 - 2x)$.
   A) $6x^2 - 6x + 8$
   B) $-6x^2 + 26x - 24$
   C) $6x^2 - 26x + 24$
   D) $-6x^2 + 26x + 24$
   E) $6x^2 + 26x - 24$

11. If 6n + m is divisible by 3 and 5, which of the following numbers when added to 6n + m will still give a result that is divisible by 3 and 5?

A) 4
B) 6
C) 12
D) 20
E) 60

12. If x is negative, and $x^3/5$ and x/5 both give the same result, what could be the value of x?

A) -5
B) -4
C) 3
D) 0
E) -1

13. If m = 3548, and n = 235, then what is the value of m * n?

A) 87940
B) 843499
C) 87900
D) 8830
E) 833780

14. A ball is thrown at a speed of 30 mph. How far will it travel in 2 minutes and 35 seconds?

A) 1.5 miles
B) 1.20 miles
C) 1.29 miles
D) 1.3 miles
E) 1.1 miles

15. Simplify: $30(\sqrt{40} - \sqrt{60})$.

A) $30(\sqrt{5} - \sqrt{15})$
B) $30(\sqrt{10} + \sqrt{15})$
C) $60(\sqrt{5} + \sqrt{15})$
D) $60(\sqrt{10} - \sqrt{15})$
E) 60

16. Simplify: $30/(\sqrt{40} - \sqrt{60})$.

A) $3(\sqrt{5} + \sqrt{15})$
B) $-3(\sqrt{5} - \sqrt{15})$
C) $-3(\sqrt{10} + \sqrt{15})$
D) $3(\sqrt{10} + \sqrt{15})$
E) $3(\sqrt{10} - \sqrt{15})$

17. What is the least common multiple of 2, 3, 4, and 5?

A) 30
B) 60
C) 120
D) 40
E) 50

18. It costs \$6 to make a pen that sells for \$12. How many pens need to be sold to make a profit of \$60?

A) 10
B) 6
C) 72
D) 30
E) 12

Math Section Question Bank: Section 4 – Answers

#1 Solution
Answer: D)
If the number is divisible by 2, d should be even.If the number is divisible by 5, then b has to equal 0.
Start by making both variables 0 and dividing by the largest factor, 7.
56800/7 = 8114.
2 from 56800 is 56798, a number divisible by 2 and 7.
Next add a multiple of 7 that turns the last number to a 0. 6 * 7 = 42. 56798 + 42 = 56840, which is divisible by 2, 5 and 7.
Skill: Algebra

#2 Solution
Answer: C)
Carla's age is c; Megan's age is m. c = 3m; c – 8 = m – 8 + 18.
Substitute 3m for c in equation 2 → 3m – 8 = m + 10 → m=9.
Skill: Algebraic Equations

#3 Solution
Answer: E)
We know $(x^2 - 25) = (x + 5)(x - 5)$.
So $(x^2 - 25)/(x + 5) = x - 5$. At $x = 0$, $f(0) = -5$.
Skill: Algebraic Equations

#4 Solution
Answer: B)
Let j be John's age and s be Sally's age.
j + 4 = 2(s + 4).
s - 8 = 10 → s = 18
So j + 4 = 2(18 + 4) → j = 40.
Skill: Algebraic Equations

#5 Solution
Answer: A)
If x is the number of marbles initially, then .25x goes to Vic, .2x goes to Robbie, and .1x goes to Jules.
The number left, x, is (1 - .25 - .2 - .1) = .45x.
Of that I give 6/20 to my brother, so 6/20 * .45x.
I am left with .45x(1 - (6/20)) = .315x.
We are also told .315x = 315 → x = 1000.
Skill: Algebraic Equations

#6 Solution

Answer: C)

Always read the question carefully! Questions 5 and 6 are similar, but they are not the same. Let x be the original number of marbles. After Vic's share is given .75x remains. After Robbie's share .75x * .80 remains. After Jules' share, .75x * .8 * .9 remains. After I give my brother his share, .75x * .8 * .9 * (1 - 6/20) remains. The remaining number = .378x. We are told .378x = 315 → x = 833.33. We need to increase this to the next highest number, 834, because we have part of a marble and to include it we need to have a whole marble.

Skill: Algebraic Equations

#7 Solution

Answer: C)

Replace the value of x with its value and solve the equation.

29 = 5y + 4.

Solving:

29 - 4 = 5y + 4 – 4.

25 = 5y or 5y = 25.

5y/5 = 25/5.

y = 5.

Skill: Algebraic Equations

#8 Solution

Answer: B)

2(8) + x > 45 means x > 29, so we need more than 29 marbles. A bag has 8 marbles, so the number of bags needed is 29/8, or 3.625. Since we need 3 bags + part of another bag, we need 4 additional bags to give at least 45 marbles.

Skill: Algebraic Equations

#9 Solution

Answer: B)

n is the number of widgets. The cost the factory incurs for making n widgets is 10000 + 50n. The amount the factory makes by selling n widgets is 550n.

At the break-even point, the cost incurred is equal to the amount of sales.

10000 + 50n = 550n → n = 20.

Skill: Algebraic Equations

#10 Solution

Answer: B)

Use FOIL:

$(3x - 4)(6 - 2x) = 3x * 6 – 4 * 6 + 3x * (-2x) – 4 * (-2x) = 18x – 24 - 6x^2 + 8x =$
$-6x^2+26x-24$.

Skill: Algebraic Equations

#11 Solution

Answer: E)

Since 6n + m is divisible by 3 and 5, the new number that we get after adding a value will be divisible by 3 and 5 only if the value that we add is divisible by 3 and 5. The only number that will work from the given choices is 60.

Skill: Algebra

#12 Solution

Answer: E)

We are told $x^3/5 = x/5 \rightarrow x^3 = x$. The possible values are -1, 0, and 1. We are told that x is negative. So x = -1.

Skill: Algebra

#13 Solution

Answer: E)

This problem can be done by elimination. We know that m is in the thousands, which means $x * 10^3$, and n is in the hundreds, which is $y * 10^2$. The answer will be $z * 10^5$, or 6 places in total, so we can eliminate A, C, and D. Also we see that m ends in 8 and n ends in 5, so the answer has to end in 0 (8*5 = 40), which eliminates B and leaves E as the only possible answer.

Skill: Algebra

#14 Solution

Answer: C)

The ball has a speed of 30 miles per hour. 30 miles per 60 minutes = .5 mile per minute. 2 minutes and 35 seconds = 2 minutes and 35/60 minutes = 2.58 minutes. The ball travels .5 * 2.58 = 1.29 miles.

Skill: Algebra

#15 Solution

Answer: D

$30(\sqrt{40} - \sqrt{60}) = 30\sqrt{4\,(10 - 15)} = 60(\sqrt{10} - \sqrt{15})$

Skill: Algebra

#16 Solution

Answer: C

Multiply the numerator and the denominator by $(\sqrt{40} + \sqrt{60})$.

So $30/(\sqrt{40} - \sqrt{60}) * [(\sqrt{40} + \sqrt{60})/(\sqrt{40} + \sqrt{60})] = 30(\sqrt{40} + \sqrt{60})/(\sqrt{40} - \sqrt{60})^2$
$= -3(\sqrt{10} + \sqrt{15})$.

Skill: Algebra

#17 Solution

Answer: B

Find all the prime numbers that multiply to give the numbers.

For 2, prime factor is 2; for 3, prime factor is 3; for 4, prime factors are 2, 2; for 5, prime factor is 5. Note the maximum times of occurrence of each prime and multiply these to find the least common multiple. The LCM is 2 * 2 * 3 * 5 = 60.

Skill: Algebra

#18 Solution

Answer: A

One pen sells for $12, so on the sale of a pen, the profit is 12 - 6 = 6.

In order to make $60, we need to sell 10 pens.

Skill: Algebra

Section 5: Inequalities, Literal Equations, Linear Systems, Polynomials, Binomials

1. If $x<5$ and $y<6$, then $x + y$ _?_ 11.
A) $<$
B) $>$
C) $\leq$
D) $\geq$
E) $=$

2. Which of the following is true about the inequality $25x^2 - 40x - 32 < 22$?
A) There are no solutions.
B) There is a set of solutions.
C) There is 1 solution only.
D) There are 2 solutions.
E) There are 3 solutions.

3. If $x - 2y > 6$, what possible values of y always have x as greater than or equal to 2?
A) $y \geq 1$
B) $y \leq 0$
C) $y \geq -2$
D) $y < 2$
E) $y \leq 6$

4. Find the point of intersection of the lines $x + 2y = 4$, and $3x - y = 26$.
A) (1, 3)
B) (8, -2)
C) (0, 2)
D) (2, -1)
E) (4, 26)

5. If $a + b = 2$, and $a - b = 4$, what is a?
A) 1
B) 2
C) 3
D) 4
E) 5

6. If $\sqrt{a} + \sqrt{b} = 2$, and $\sqrt{a} - \sqrt{b} = 3$, what is a+b?
A) 6.5
B) 6
C) 5.5
D) 5
E) 4.5

7. If a = b + 3, and 3b = 5a + 6, what is 3a - 2b?
A) -1.5
B) 2.5
C) 3
D) 4.3
E) 5

8. The sum of the roots of a quadratic equation is 8, and the difference is 2. What is the equation?
A) $x^2 - 8x - 15$
B) $x^2 + 8x + 15$
C) $x^2 - 8x + 15$
D) $x^2 + 8x - 15$
E) $x^2 + 15$

9. Solve the following system of equations: 3x + 2y = 7 and 3x + y = 5.
A) x = 2, y = 1
B) x = 2, y = 2
C) x = 1, y = 0
D) x = 1, y = 2
E) x = 1, y = 1

10. Nine tickets were sold for $41. If the tickets cost $4 and $5, how many $5 tickets were sold?
A) 5
B) 4
C) 9
D) 6
E) 7

11. Joe brought a bag of 140 M&Ms to his class of 40 students. Each boy received 2 M&Ms. Each girl received 4. How many boys were in the class?
A) 10
B) 20
C) 30
D) 40
E) 50

Math Section Question Bank: Section 5 – Answers

#1 Solution
Answer: A)
Choice A will always be true, while the other choices can never be true.
Skill: Inequalities

#2 Solution
Answer: B)
$25x^2 - 40x + 32 < 22 \rightarrow 25x^2 - 40x + 16 < 6 \rightarrow (5x - 4)^2 < 6 \rightarrow 5x - 4 < 6$.
$x = 2$, so x has to be all numbers less than 2 for this inequality to work.
Skill: Inequalities

#3 Solution
Answer: C)
Rearrange equation $x > 6 + 2y$, so $2 > 6 + 2y$. Solve for y.
$2 \geq 6 + 2y$.
$-4 \geq 2y$, so $-2 \leq y$ or $y \geq -2$.
(When working with inequalities, remember to reverse the sign when dividing by a negative number.)
Skill: Inequalities

#4 Solution
Answer: B)
Find the slopes first. If they are not equal, then the lines intersect. The slopes are -1/2 and 3.
Next, solve by substitution or addition. From the first equation, $x = 4 - 2y$. Plugging this into equation 2, we get $3(4 - 2y) - y = 26 \rightarrow 7y = 12 - 26 \rightarrow y = -2$. Plug this value into either equation to find x. With equation 1, we get $x - 4 = 4 \rightarrow x = 8$.
Skill: Linear Systems

#5 Solution
Answer: C)
Add the equations to eliminate b. $2a = 6 \rightarrow a = 3$.
Skill: Linear Systems

#6 Solution
Answer: A)
Square both equations.
Equation 1 becomes $a + 2\sqrt{ab} + b = 4$ and equation 2 becomes $a - 2\sqrt{ab} + b = 9$.
Add the equations. $2(a + b) = 13 \rightarrow a + b = 13/2$. $13/2 = 6.5$.
Skill: Linear Systems

#7 Solution

Answer: A)

Solve by substitution.

$$3b = 5(b+3) + 6 \qquad a = -10.5 + 3 = -7.5$$

$$3b - 5b - 15 = 6$$

$$-2b = 21 \quad b = -10.5 \qquad 3(-7.5) - 2(-10.5) = -1.5$$

Skill: Linear Systems

#8 Solution

Answer: C)

If the roots are a and b, then a + b = 8 and a - b = 2.
Add the equations. 2a = 10 → a = 5 → b = 3.
The factors are (x - 5)(x - 3), and the equation is $x^2 - 8x + 15$.
Skill: Linear Systems

#9 Solution

Answer: D)

From the equation 3x + y = 5, we get y = 5 - 3x. Substitute into the other equation.
3x + 2(5 - 3x) = 7 → 3x + 10 - 6x = 7 → x = 1. This value into either of the equations gives us y = 2.
Skill: Linear Systems

#10 Solution

Answer: A)

4x + 5y = 41, and x + y = 9, where x and y are the number of tickets sold.
From equation 2: x = 9 - y. From equation 1: 4(9 - y) + 5y = 41 → 36 + y = 41 → y = 5.
Skill: Linear Systems

#11 Solution

Answer: A)

b is the number of boys. g is the number of girls.
So b + g = 40, and 2b + 4g = 140.
To do the problem, use the substitution method. From equation 1, g = 40 - b.
Plug this into equation 2. So 2b + 4(40 - b) = 140→b = 10.
Skill: Linear Systems

Section 6: Slope, Distance to Midpoint, Graphing, Linear Equations

1. What is the equation of the line that passes through (3, 5) with intercept $y = 8$?
A) $y = x + 8$
B) $y = x - 8$
C) $y = -x - 8$
D) $y = -x + 8$
E) $y = -x$

2. What is the value of y in the equation $(3x - 4)^2 = 4y - 15$, if $x = 3$?
A) 10
B) 2.5
C) -10
D) -2.5
E) 5

3. If $y = 4x + 6y$, what is the range of y if $-10 < x \leq 5$?
A) $-4 < y \leq 8$
B) $-4 < y < 8$
C) $8 > y > -4$
D) $-4 \leq y < 8$
E) $-4 \leq y \leq 8$

4. If Jennifer gets three times as much allowance as Judy gets, and Judy gets $5/week, how much does Jennifer get every month?
A) $15
B) $20
C) $30
D) $45
E) $60

5. What is the value of x, if $y = 8$ in the equation $5x + 9y = 3x - 6y + 5$?
A) 57.5
B) 60
C) -60
D) -57.5
E) None of the above.

6. What is the area outside the circle, but within the square whose two corners are A and B?

A (3, 5) B (8, 17)

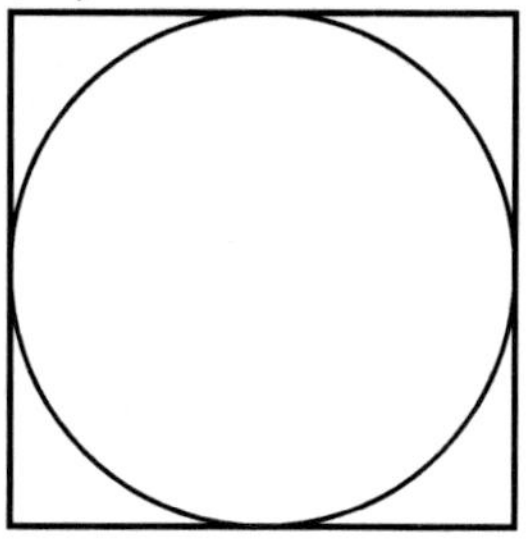

A) 169(1-π)
B) 169 π
C) 169 π /4
D) 169(1- π /4)
E) 169

7. Determine where the following two lines intersect:

$$3x + 4y = 7$$
$$9x + 12y = 21$$

A) x = 4, y = 3
B) x = 12, y = 9
C) x = 1/3, y = 1/3
D) Not enough information provided.
E) There is no solution; the lines do not intersect.

8. A line with a slope of 2 passes through the point (2, 4). What is the set of coordinates where that line passes through the y intercept?
A) (-2,0)
B) (0,0)
C) (2,2)
D) (4,0)
E) (1,1)

9. Are the following lines parallel or perpendicular?

$$3x + 4y = 7$$
$$8x - 6y = 9$$

A) Parallel.
B) Perpendicular.
C) Neither parallel nor perpendicular.
D) Cannot be determined.
E) The angle at the point of intersection is 40.

10. Is the graph of the function $f(x) = -3x^2 + 4$ linear, asymptotical, symmetrical to the x axis, symmetrical to the y axis, or not symmetrical to either axis?

A) Symmetrical to the x axis.
B) Symmetrical to the y axis.
C) Symmetrical to neither axis.
D) Asymptotic.
E) Linear.

11. Two points on a line have coordinates (3, 12) and (9, 20). What is the distance between these two points?

A) 10
B) 12
C) 13
D) 8
E) 11

12. In the following graph, what is the equation of line AB if line AB is perpendicular to line PQ? Point coordinates are:

M (-4,0), O (0,2), N (0,-3). The lines intersect at (-2,1).

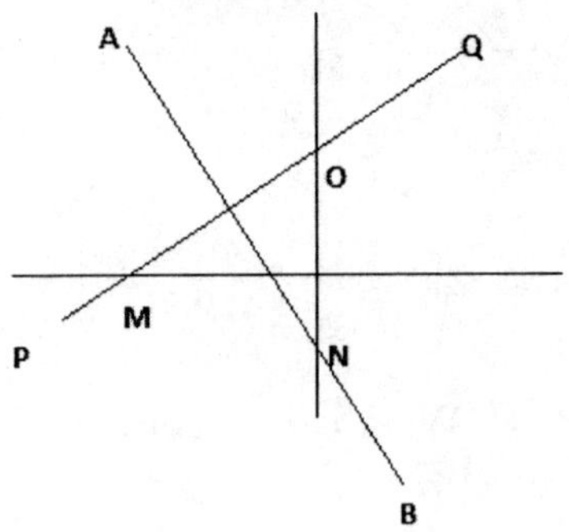

A) $y = 2x + 3$
B) $y = -2x - 3$
C) $y = x - 4$
D) $y = x + 3$
E) $y = -2x - 3$

13. What is the equation of a line passing through (1, 2) and (6, 12)?

A) $y = x$
B) $y = 2x$
C) $y = x/2$
D) $y = 2x+2$
E) $y = x-2$

14. What is the midpoint of the line connecting points (0, 8) and (2, 6)?
A) (-1, 1)
B) (2, 14)
C) (-2, 2)
D) (0, 1)
E) (1, 7)

15. What is the equation of a line passing through (1, 1) and (2, 4)?
A) 3y = x + 2
B) 2y = x + 3
C) y = 3x - 2
D) 4x = y + 2
E) y = (1/3)x + 2

16. Line A passes through (0, 0) and (3, 4). Line B passes through (2, 6) and (3, y). What value of y will make the lines parallel?
A) 20/3
B) 7
C) 22/3
D) 29
E) 5

17. Line A passes through (1, 3) and (3, 4). Line B passes through (3, 7) and (5, y). What value of y will make the lines perpendicular?
A) 1
B) 2
C) 3
D) 4
E) 5

18. What is the equation of line A that is perpendicular to line B, connecting (8, 1) and (10, 5), that intersects at (x, 14)?
A) y = 2x – 7
B) y = -2x + 7
C) y = (-1/2)x + $19\frac{1}{4}$
D) y = 5x – 7
E) y = 2x - $19\frac{1}{4}$

Math Section Question Bank: Section 6 – Answers

#1 Solution

Answer: D)

The standard form of the line equation is $y = mx + b$.

We need to find slope m. $m = (y_2 - y_1)/(x_2 - x_1) \rightarrow m = (5 - 8)/(3 - 0) \rightarrow m = -1$.

Therefore the equation is $y = -x + 8$.

Skill: Linear Equations

#2 Solution

Answer: A)

At $x = 3$, $((3 \cdot 3) - 4)^2 = 4y - 15$

$(9 - 4)^2 = 4y - 15$

$25 = 4y - 15$

$40 = 4y$

$y = 10$

Skill: Literal Equations

#3 Solution

Answer: D)

Rearrange the equation and combine like terms. $-5y = 4x$.

At $x = -10$, $y = 8$. At $x = 5$, $y = -4$. The range of y is therefore $-4 \leq y < 8$.

Skill: Literal equations

#4 Solution

Answer: E)

If Judy gets x dollars, then Jennifer gets 3x in a week. In a month, Jennifer will then get 4 * 3x.

If Judy gets $5 per week, then Jennifer gets $60 in a month.

Skill: Literal equation

#5 Solution

Answer: D)

Combine like terms.

$5x + 9y = 3x - 6y + 5 \rightarrow 2x = -15y + 5 \rightarrow x = -57.5$ when $y = 8$.

Skill: Literal equations

#6 Solution

Answer: D)

First we need to find the length of side AB. $AB = \sqrt{(17 - 5)^2 + (8 - 3)^2} = 13$.

If $AB = 13$, then $A_{square} = 13^2 = 169$.

AB is also the diameter of the circle. $A_{circle}\ \pi\ (d^2/4) = 169\ \pi\ /4$.

The area outside the circle and within the square is:

$A_{square} - A_{circle} = 169(1 - \pi\ /4)$.

Skill: Geometry & Slope, Distance, Graphing

#7 Solution

Answer: E)

While it is tempting to solve this system of simultaneous equations to find the values of x and y, the first thing to do is to see whether the lines intersect. To do this, compare the slopes of the two lines by putting the lines into the standard form, $y = mx + b$, where m is the slope.

By rearranging, equation 1 becomes $y = 7/4 - 3x/4$ and equation 2 becomes $y = 21/12 - 9x/12$.

The slope of line 1 is -3/4, and the slope of line 2 is -9/12, which reduces to -3/4. Since the slopes are equal, the lines are parallel and do not intersect.

Skill: Slope, Distance to Midpoint, Graphing

#8 Solution

Answer: B)

The slope of the line is given as $m = (y_2 - y_1)/(x_2 - x_1)$, where (x_1,y_1) and (x_2,y_2) are two points which the line passes through. The y intercept is the point where the graph intersects the y axis, so $x = 0$ at this point.

Plugging in the values of m, etc., we get $2 = (4 - y)/(2 - 0) \rightarrow y = 0$.

Skill: Slope, Distance to Midpoint, Graphing

#9 Solution

Answer: B)

Find the slopes by rearranging the two equations into the form $y = mx + b$.

Equation 1 becomes $y = -3x/4 + 7/4$ and equation 2 becomes $y = 8x/6 - 9/6$.

So $m_1 = -3/4$ and $m_2 = 8/6 = 4/3$. We see that m_1 is the negative inverse of m_2, so line 1 is perpendicular to line 2.

Skill: Slope, Distance to Midpoint, Graphing

#10 Solution

Answer: B)

Find the values of the y coordinate for different values of the x coordinate (example, [-3, +3]). We get the following chart:

x	y
-3	-23
-2	-8
-1	1
0	4
1	1
2	-8
3	-23

From these values, we see the graph is symmetrical to the y axis.

Skill: Slope, Distance to Midpoint, Graphing

#11 Solution
Answer: A)
Distance $s = \sqrt{(x_2 - x_1)^2 + (y_2 - y_1)^2} \rightarrow s = \sqrt{(9 - 3)^2 + (20 - 12)^2} = \sqrt{36 + 64} = 10$.
Skill: Slope, Distance to Midpoint, Graphing

#12 Solution
Answer: B)
y = mx + b; m is the slope and b is the y intercept. Calculate m for line AB using the given points (0, -3) and (-2, 1). m = (-3 -1)/(0-(-2)) = -2. The y intercept is -3 (from point set given), so y = -2x - 3.
Skill: Slope, Distance to Midpoint, Graphing

#13 Solution
Answer: B)
First, find the slope, $(y_2-y_1)/(x_2-x_1) \rightarrow$ slope = (12 - 2)/(6 - 1) = 2.
Next, use the slope and a point to find the value of b.
In the standard line equation, y = mx + b, use the point (6, 12) to get
12 = (2 * 6) + b → b = 0.
The equation of the line is y = 2x.
Skill: Slope, Distance to Midpoint, Graphing

#14 Solution
Answer: E)
The midpoint is at $(x_1 + x_2)/2,(y_1 + y_2)/2 = (1,7)$.
Skill: Slope, Distance to Midpoint, Graphing

#15 Solution
Answer: C)
Slope = $(y_2 - y_1)/(x_2 - x_1) = 3$. Plug one of the coordinates into y = mx + b to find the value of b.
1 = 3(1) + b → b = - 2.
The equation of the line is y = 3x - 2.
Skill: Slope, Distance to Midpoint, Graphing

#16 Solution
Answer: C)
Calculate the slope of each line. Slope of line A = 4/3 and slope of line B = y - 6.
The slopes of the line have to be the same for the lines to be parallel.
4/3 = y – 6 → 4 = 3y – 18 → y = 22/3.
Skill: Slope, Distance to Midpoint, Graphing

#17 Solution

Answer: C)

The slope of line A = 1/2 and the slope of line B = (y - 7)/2.
The product of the slopes has to equal -1.
(1/2)[(y - 7)/2] = -1 → (y - 7)/4 = -1 → y = 3.
Skill: Slope, Distance to Midpoint, Graphing

#18 Solution

Answer: C)

$Slope_b$ = (5 - 1)/(10 - 8) = 2. The slope of line A is -1/2.
To find the intercept of line B, use y = mx + b.
5 = (2)(10) + b, so b = -7. Equation of line B is y = 2x – 7.
Find the intersect x using the given y coordinate. 14 = 2x – 7; x = 10.5.
Find the intercept of line A using the coordinates of intersection.
14 = (-1/2)(10.5)+b. b = $19\frac{1}{4}$.
The equation of line A is y = - (1/2)x + $19\frac{1}{4}$.
Skill: Geometry & Slope

Section 7: Quadratics, Functions, Absolute Value Equations, Dividing Equations

1. Factor $x^2+2x-15$.
A) $(x - 3)(x + 5)$
B) $(x + 3)(x - 5)$
C) $(x + 3)(x + 5)$
D) $(x - 3)(x - 5)$
E) $(x - 1)(x + 15)$

2. Car A starts at 3:15 PM and travels straight to its destination at a constant speed of 50 mph. If it arrives at 4:45 PM, how far did it travel?
A) 70 miles
B) 75 miles
C) 65 miles
D) 40 miles
E) 105 miles

3. What are the roots of the equation $2x^2+14x = 0$?
A) 0 and 7
B) 0 and -7
C) 14 and 0
D) 2 and 14
E) Cannot be determined.

4. If $f(x) = 2x^2 + 3x$, and $g(x) = x + 4$, what is $f[g(x)]$?
A) $x^2 + 19x + 44$
B) $2x^2 + 19x + 44$
C) $4x^2 + 35x + 76$
D) $x^2 + 8x + 16$
E) None of the above.

5. If $|x + 4| = 2$, what are the values of x?
A) 2 and 6
B) -2 and -6
C) -2
D) -6
E) 0

6. The sale of an item can be written as a function of price: $s = 3p + c$, where s is the amount in sales, p is the price charged per item, and c is a constant value. If the sales generated are \$20 at a price of \$5 for the item, then what should the price be to generate \$50 in sales?

A) \$10
B) \$15
C) \$20
D) \$16
E) \$14

7. If $f(n) = 2n + 3\sqrt{n}$, where n is a positive integer, what is $f[g(5)]$ if $g(m) = m - 4$?

A) 1
B) 2
C) 3
D) 4
E) 5

8. If $f(x) = (x + 2)^2$, and $-4 \leq x \leq 4$, what is the minimum value of f(x)?

A) 0
B) 1
C) 2
D) 3
E) 4

9. If $f(x) = (x + 2)^2$, and $0 \leq x \leq 4$, what is the minimum value of f(x)?

A) 1
B) 2
C) 3
D) 4
E) 5

10. What is $x^2 - 9$ divided by $x - 3$?

A) $x - 3$
B) $x + 3$
C) x
D) $x - 1$
E) 6

11. What is $x^4 + 3x^3 + 4x$ divided by $x^2 + 3$?

A) $x^2 + 3x + \frac{3x^2-5x}{x^2+3}$
B) $x^2 + 3 - 3 + \frac{9-5x}{x^2+3}$
C) x^2
D) $x^2 + 3x$
E) 3x

12. An equation has two roots: 5 and -8. What is a possible equation?
A) $x^2 - 3x + 40$
B) $x^2 - 3x - 40$
C) $x^2 + x + 40$
D) $x^2 + 3x - 40$
E) $2x^2 - 3x + 40$

13. In an ant farm, the number of ants grows every week according to the formula $N = 100 + 2^w$, where w is the number of weeks elapsed. How many ants will the colony have after 5 weeks?
A) 115
B) 125
C) 135
D) 132
E) 233

14. Find the values of x that validate the following equation:
$[(4x + 5)^2 - (40x + 25)]^{1/2} + 3|x| - 14 = 0.$
A) -2, -14
B) 2, -14
C) -2, 14
D) 2, 14
E) No solution

15. If $|x| = 4$ and $|y| = 5$, what are the values of $|x + y|$?
A) 1, 9
B) -1, 9
C) -1, -9
D) -1, -9
E) $1<|x + y| < 9$

16. If $y = |x|$, what is the range of y?

A) $y < 0$
B) $0 < y < x$
C) $y > 0$
D) $y \geq 0$
E) $y > x$

Math Section Question Bank: Section 7 – Answers

#1 Solution
Answer: A)
The constant term is -15. The factors should multiply to give -15 and add to give 2. The numbers -3 and 5 satisfy both, (x - 3)(x + 5).
Skill: Quadratics

#2 Solution
Answer: B)
The time between 3:15 PM and 4:45 PM = 1.5 hours. 1.5 * 50 = 75.
Reminder: half an hour is written as .5 of an hour, not .3 of an hour, even though on a clock a half hour is 30 minutes.
Skill: Functions

#3 Solution
Answer: B)
Rearrange, reduce, and factor.

$2x^2 + 14x + 0 = 0$
$2(x^2 + 7x + 0) = 0$
$(x + 7)(x + 0)$
$x = 0 \quad \text{or} \quad -7$

Skill: Quadratic Equations

#4 Solution
Answer: B)
Substitute g(x) for every x in f(x).
$f[g((x + 4))] = 2(x + 4)^2 + 3(x + 4) = 2x^2 + 16x + 32 + 3x + 12 = 2x^2 + 19x + 44$
Skill: Functions

#5 Solution
Answer: B)
Two solutions: (x + 4) = 2 and –(x + 4) = 2.
Or x + 4 = 2, x = -2.
And x + 4 = -2, x = -6.
Skill: Absolute Value Equations

#6 Solution
Answer: B)
Find the value of the constant by plugging in the given information.
20 = 3 * 5 + c → c = 5.
Now use the value of c and the new value of s to find p.50 = 3p + 5 → p = 15.
Skill: Functions

#7 Solution
Answer: E)
$g(5) = 5 - 4 = 1$. $f[g(5)] = 2 * 1 + 3\sqrt{1} = 5$.
Skill: Functions

#8 Solution
Answer: A)
From the domain of x, the lowest value of x is -4, and the highest value is 4. We are tempted to think that f(x) will have the least value at x = -4: f(-4) = 4. However, f(x) is equal to a squared value, so the lowest value of f(x) is 0. This happens at x = -2.
Skill: Functions

#9 Solution
Answer: D)
The lowest value of f(x) can be 0, since f(x) is equal to a squared value, but, for f(x) = 0, x must equal -2 That is outside the domain of x. The least value of f(x) = 4.
Skill: Functions

#10 Solution
Answer: B)
$x^2 - 9$ can be factored into (x + 3) and (x - 3).
[(x + 3)(x - 3)]/(x - 3) = x + 3
Skill: Dividing Equations

#11 Solution
Answer: B)

$$\begin{array}{r} x^2+3x-3 \\ x^2+3\,\overline{)\,x^4+3x^3+0x^2+4x+0} \\ \underline{x^4 \qquad\quad +3x^2} \\ 3x^3-3x^2+4x \\ \underline{3x^3 \qquad\quad +9x} \\ -3x^2-5x \\ \underline{-3x^2 \qquad\quad -9} \\ -5x-9 \end{array}$$

Skill: Dividing Equations

#12 Solution

Answer: D)

If the roots are 5 and -8, the factors are (x - 5)(x + 8). Multiply the factors to get the equation.

$x^2 + 3x - 40$

Skill: Quadratic Equations

#13 Solution

Answer: D)

After 5 weeks, the number of ants = 100 + 32, or132.

Skill: Function

#14 Solution

Answer: D)

Expand the equation:

$[16x^2 + 40x + 25 - 40x - 25]^{1/2} + 3|x| - 14 = 0$

$(16x^2)^{1/2} + 3|x| - 14 = 0$

$4x + 3|x| - 14 = 0$

$3|x| = 14 - 4x$

$|x| = \frac{14}{3} - \frac{4x}{3}$ $\quad$ $x = \frac{14}{3} - \frac{4x}{3} = 2$ $\quad$ $x = -\frac{14}{3} - \frac{4x}{3} = 14$

Skill: Absolute Value Equations

#15 Solution

Answer: A)

x = 4 and y = 5, $|x + y| = 9$

x = -4 and y = 5, $|x + y| = 1$

x = 4 and y = -5, $|x + y| = 1$

x = -4 and y = -5, $|x + y| = 9$

Skill: Absolute Value Equations

#16 Solution

Answer: D)

The absolute value of x can be at least a 0, and is otherwise positive regardless of the value of x.

$y \geq 0$

Skill: Absolute Value

Section 8: Geometry

1. What is the area outside the circle, but within the square whose two corners are A and B?

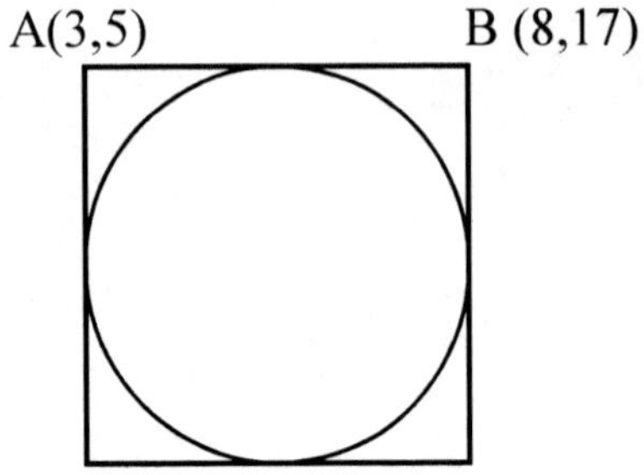

A) 169(1- π)
B) 169 π
C) 169 π /4
D) 169(1- π /4)
E) 169

2. What is the area, in square feet, of the triangle whose sides have lengths equal to 3, 4, and 5 feet?
A) 6 square feet
B) 7 square feet
C) 4 square feet
D) 5 square feet
E) 8 square feet

3. In the following figure, where AE bisects line BC, and angles AEC and AEB are both right angles, what is the length of AB?

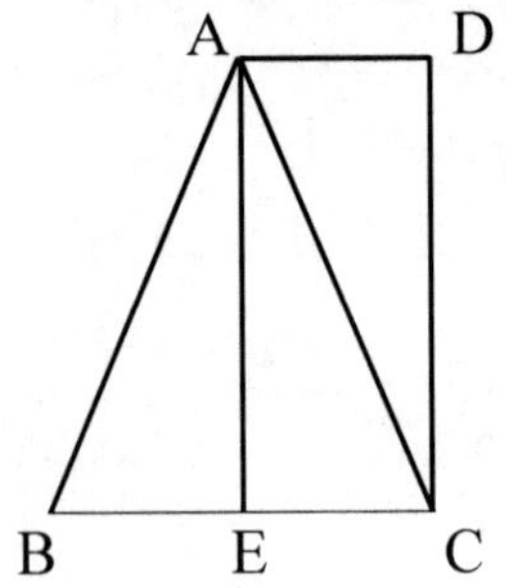

BC = 6 cm
AD = 3 cm
CD = 4 cm

A) 1 cm
B) 2 cm
C) 3 cm
D) 4 cm
E) 5 cm

4. In the following triangle, if AB = 6 and BC = 8, what should the length of CA be to make triangle ABC a right triangle?

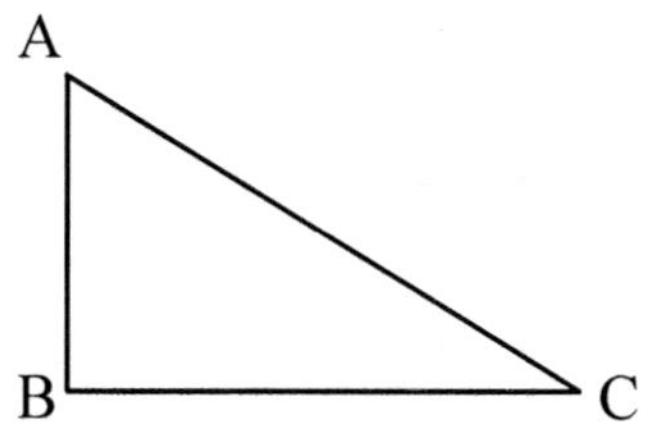

A) 10
B) 9
C) 8
D) 4
E) 7

5. In the following circle there is a square with an area of 36 cm^2. What is the area outside the square, but within the circle?

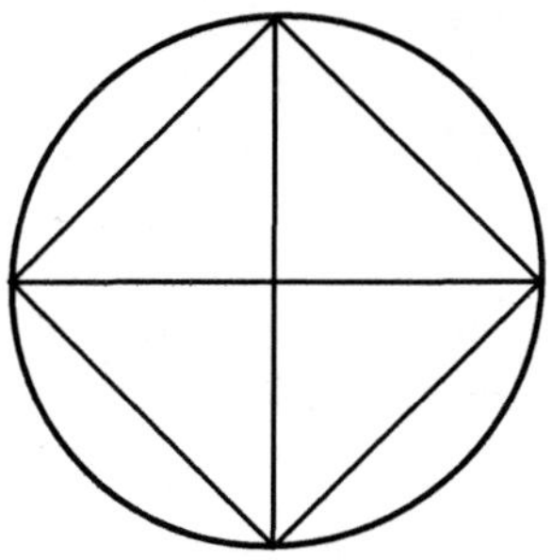

A) $18\pi\ cm^2$
B) $18\pi - 30\ cm^2$
C) $18\pi - 36\ cm^2$
D) $18\ cm^2$
E) $-18\ cm^2$

6. If a square of area 25 cm^2 is rotated around the side AB, what is the volume of the resulting shape?
A) 625
B) 625π
C) 125π
D) $25\pi^2$
E) $625\pi^2$

7. The length of a rectangle is 4 times its width. If the width of the rectangle is 5 - x inches and the perimeter of the rectangle is 30 inches, what is x?
A) 1
B) 2
C) 3
D) 4
E) 5

8. If in triangle ABC, AB:AC = 6:10, then what is BC/AC?

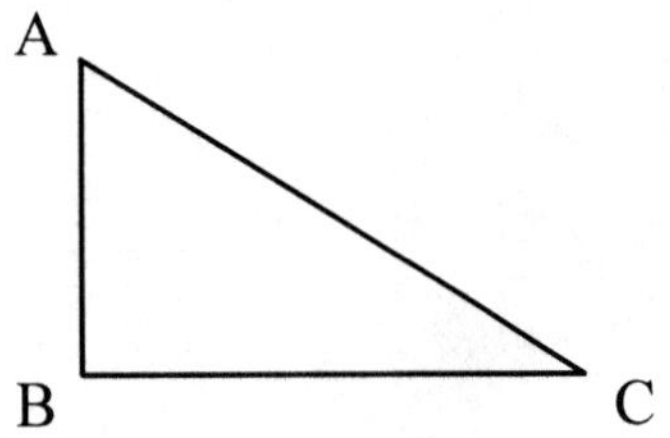

A) 8:10
B) 6:8
C) 4:5
D) 2:5
E) 5:8

9. Two sides of a triangle have a ratio AC:BC = 5:4. The length of AB on a similar triangle = 24. What is the actual value of AC for the larger triangle?

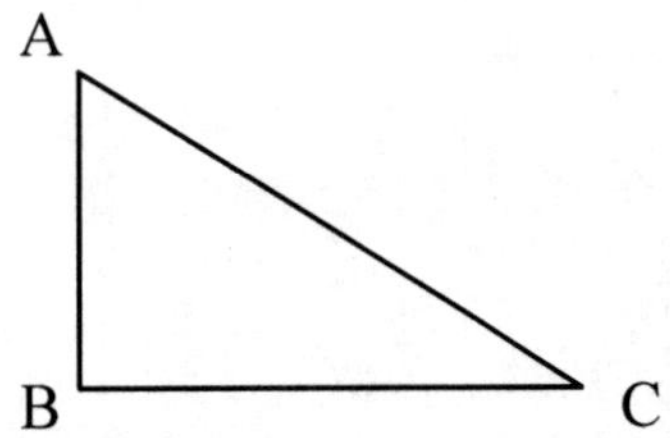

A) 10
B) 14.4
C) 35
D) 40
E) 50

10. If the diameter of a circle is doubled, the area increases by what factor?
A) 1 time
B) 2 times
C) 3 times
D) 4 times
E) 5 times

11. A rectangular prism's length = 4 cm, width = 5 cm, and height = 10 cm. It weighs 6 kg. If the length is cut in half, the width is doubled, and the height stays the same, how much will the resulting rectangular prism weigh?

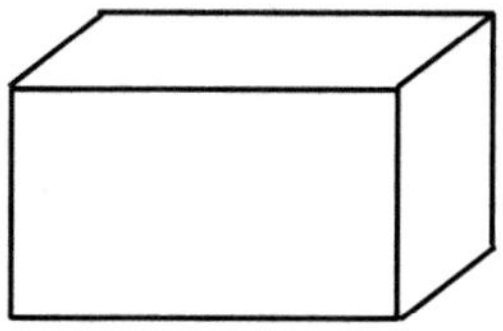

A) 6 kg
B) 3 kg
C) 200 g
D) 400 g
E) 5 kg

12. In the following figure, what is A?

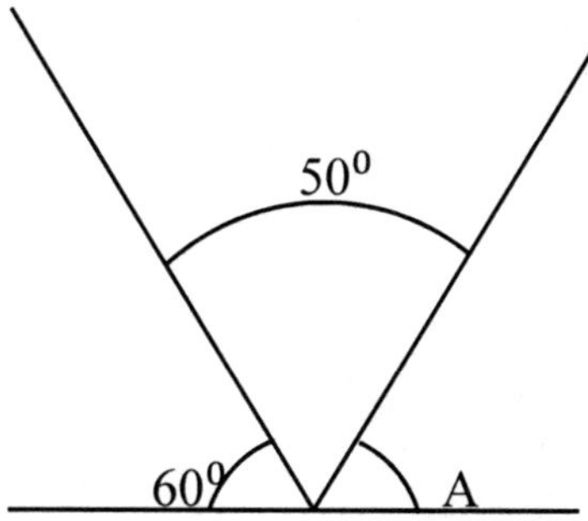

A) 110^0
B) 70^0
C) 180^0
D) 50^0
E) 55^0

13. In the following isosceles triangle, what is the largest possible value of angle B?

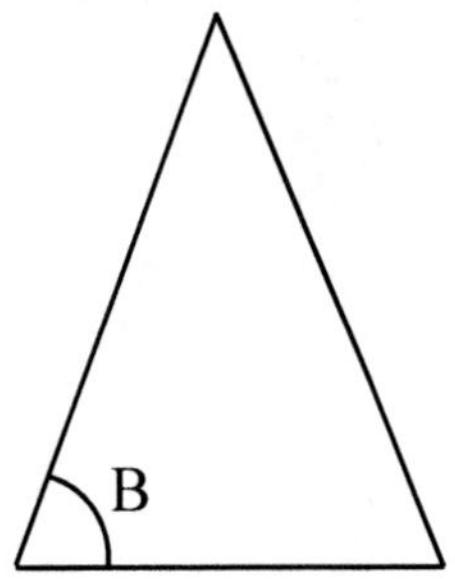

A) 59.5^0
B) 45.0^0
C) 90.0^0
D) 89.5^0
E) 30.5^0

14. In the following figure, what are the values of angles A, B and C?

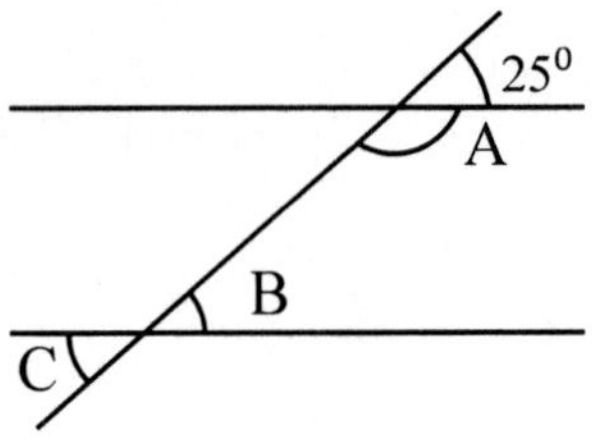

A) $\angle A = 155^0$, $\angle B = 25^0$, $\angle C = 25^0$
B) $\angle A = 145^0$, $\angle B = 20^0$, $\angle C = 20^0$
C) $\angle A = 150^0$, $\angle B = 25^0$, $\angle C = 25^0$
D) $\angle A = 55^0$, $\angle B = 35^0$, $\angle C = 45^0$
E) $\angle A = 155^0$, $\angle B = 35^0$, $\angle C = 25^0$

15. In the following triangle PQR, what is the measure of angle A?

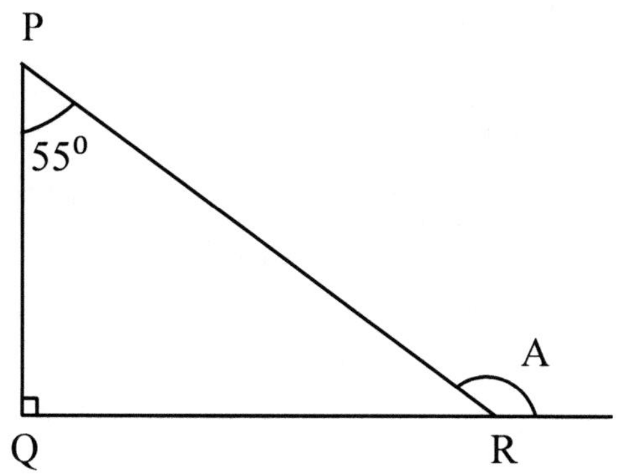

A) 145^0
B) 140^0
C) 70^0
D) 50^0
E) 40^0

16. In the triangle ABC, the length of AB = 5 and the length of BC = 7. Which of the following cannot be the length of AC?
A) 3
B) 6
C) 11
D) 12
E) 10

Math Section Question Bank: Section 8 – Answers

#1 Solution

Answer: D)

First find the length of side AB. AB = $\sqrt{(17-5)2+(8-3)2}$ = 13.
If AB = 13, then A_{square} = 132 = 169.
AB is also the diameter of the circle, so A_{circle} π $(d^2/4)$ = 169 π /4.
The area outside the circle, but within the square is:
$A_{square} - A_{circle}$ = 169(1- π /4).
Skill: Geometry & Slope, Distance, Graphing

#2 Solution

Answer: A)

The Pythagorean triple (special right triangle property) means the two shorter sides form a right triangle.
1/2bh = A.
(1/2)(3)(4) = 6.
Skill: Geometry

#3 Solution

Answer: E)

$AB^2 = AC^2$ = AD2 + CD^2 → $AB^2 = 3^2 + 4^2$ → AB = 5.
Skill: Geometry

#4 Solution

Answer: A)

In a right triangle, the square of the hypotenuse = the sum of the squares of the other two sides. $AB^2 + BC^2 = AC^2$ → $AC^2 = 36 + 64$ → AC = 10.
Skill: Geometry

#5 Solution

Answer: C)

If the area of the square is 36 cm^2, then each side is 6 cm. If we look at the triangle made by half the square, that diagonal would be the hypotenuse of the triangle, and its length = $\sqrt{6^2+6^2} = 6\sqrt{2}$.
This hypotenuse is also the diameter of the circle, so the radius of the circle is $3\sqrt{2}$.
The area of the circle $= A = \pi r^2$ = 18π.
The area outside the square, but within the circle is 18π -36.
Skill: Geometry

#6 Solution

Answer: C)

If the area of the square is 25 cm^2, then a side will be 5 cm. If the square is rotated around side AB, which is 5 cm, then the top of the square will sweep a circular area of radius 5 cm to form a three dimensional cylinder. Volume of a cylinder:
$V = \pi * r^2 * h = (5^2) * 5 * \pi = 125\pi$.
Skill: Geometry

#7 Solution

Answer: B)

Perimeter of a rectangle = 2(l + w).
Width = 5 - x and length = 4(5 - x).
Perimeter = 2(l * w) = 30 → 2(20 - 4x + 5 - x) = 30 → -10x = -20 → x = 2.
Skill: Geometry

#8 Solution

Answer: A)

If the ratio of AB:AC = 6:10, then this ratio is always constant, regardless of the actual value of AB or AC.
Assuming that AB = 6 and AC = 8, BC = $\sqrt{(AC^2 - AB^2)}$ = 8.
BC:AC = 8:10, which is still a ratio, so it does not matter what the actual values are.
Skill: Geometry

#9 Solution

Answer: D)

Side AC = 5 and side BC = 4. The Pythagorean triple is 3:4:5, so side AB = 3.
Because the other triangle is similar, the ratio of all sides is constant. AB:AB = 3:24.
The ratio factor is 8. AC of the larger triangle = 5 * 8 = 40.
Skill: Geometry

#10 Solution

Answer: D)

The area of a circle = $\pi * r^2$.
If the diameter is doubled, then the radius is also doubled.
The new area = $\pi * (2r)^2 = 4 * \pi * r^2$. The area increases four times.
Skill: Geometry

#11 Solution

Answer: A)

Original $volume_{4,5,10}$ = 4 * 5 * 10 = 200 cm^3.
New $volume_{2,10,10}$ = 2 * 10 * 10 = 200 cm^3.
If 1 cm^3 is 30 gm, then 200 cm^3 will be 6000 gm = 6 kg.
Skill: Geometry

#12 Solution

Answer: B)

The angle of a straight line = 180^0.

$60^0 + 50^0 + \angle A = 180^0 \rightarrow \angle A = 70^0$.

Skill: Geometry

#13 Solution

Answer: D)

The sum of the three angles of a triangle = 180^0. According to the definition of an isosceles triangle, the two angles that are opposite the two equal sides are also equal. The third angle has to be at least 1^0. The sum of the other two angles = 180-1, or 179^0. Half of $179^0 = 89.5^0$.

Skill: Geometry

#14 Solution

Answer: A)

$\angle A + 25^0 = 180^0$; $\angle A = 155^0$ (Supplementary Angles).

$\angle B = 25^0$ (Corresponding Angles).

$\angle B = \angle C$; $\angle C = 25^0$ (Opposite Angles).

Skill: Geometry

#15 Solution

Answer: A)

$\angle P = 55^0$. $\angle Q = 90^0$. $\angle R = 180-(55+90) = 35^0$, and $\angle A = 180 - 35 = 145^0$.

Skill: Geometry

#16 Solution

Answer: D)

In any triangle, the sum of two sides must be greater than the length of the third side. The sum of the given sides = 12. The third side has to be less than 12.

Skill: Geometry

Section 9: Fundamental Counting Principle, Permutations, Combinations

1. The wardrobe of a studio contains 4 hats, 3 suits, 5 shirts, 2 pants, and 3 pairs of shoes. How many different ways can these items be put together?
   A) 60
   B) 300
   C) 360
   D) 420
   E) 500

2. For lunch, you have a choice between chicken fingers or cheese sticks for an appetizer; turkey, chicken, or veal for the main course; cake or pudding for dessert; and either Coke or Pepsi for a beverage. How many choices of possible meals do you have?
   A) 16
   B) 24
   C) 34
   D) 36
   E) 8

3. For an office job, I need to pick 3 candidates out of a pool of 5. How many choices do I have?
   A) 60
   B) 20
   C) 10
   D) 30
   E) 50

4. A contractor is supposed to choose 3 tiles out of a stack of 5 tiles to make as many patterns as possible. How many different patterns can he make?
   A) 10
   B) 20
   C) 30
   D) 40
   E) 60

5. I have chores to do around the house on a weekend. There are 5 chores I must complete by the end of the day. I can choose to do them in any order, so long as they are all completed. How many choices do I have?
   A) 5
   B) 25
   C) 32
   D) 3125
   E) 120

6. Next weekend, I have more chores to do around the house. There are 5 chores I must complete by the end of the day. I can choose to do any 2 of them in any order, and then do any 2 the next day again in any order, and then do the remaining 1 the following day. How many choices do I have?
   A) 20
   B) 6
   C) 120
   D) 130
   E) 25

7. A certain lottery play sheet has 10 numbers from which 5 have to be chosen. How many different ways can I pick the numbers?
   A) 150
   B) 250
   C) 252
   D) 143
   E) 278

8. At a buffet, there are 3 choices for an appetizer, 6 choices for a beverage, and 3 choices for an entrée. How many different ways can I select food from all the food choices?
   A) 12
   B) 27
   C) 36
   D) 42
   E) 54

9. If there is a basket of 10 assorted fruits, and I want to pick out 3 fruits, how many combinations of fruits do I have to choose from?
   A) 130
   B) 210
   C) 310
   D) 120
   E) 100

10. How many ways can I pick 3 numbers from a set of 10 numbers?
   A) 720
   B) 120
   C) 180
   D) 150
   E) 880

Math Section Question Bank: Section 9 – Answers

#1 Solution
Answer: C)
The number of ways = 4 * 3 * 5 * 2 * 3 = 360.
Skill: Fundamental Counting Principle

#2 Solution
Answer: B)
Multiply the possible number of choices for each item from which you can choose.
2 * 3 * 2 * 2 = 24.
Skill: Fundamental Counting Principle

#3 Solution
Answer: C)
This is a combination problem. The order of the candidates does not matter. The number of combinations = 5!/3!(5 - 3)! = 5 * 4/2 * 1 = 10.
Skill: Combinations

#4 Solution
Answer: E)
This is a permutation problem. The order in which the tiles are arranged is counted.
The number of patterns = 5!/(5 - 3)! = 5 * 4 * 3 = 60.
Skill: Permutation

#5 Solution
Answer: E)
This is a permutation problem. The order in which the chores are completed matters.
$^5P_5$ = 5!/(5 - 5)! = 5! = 5 * 4 * 3 * 2 * 1 = 120.
Skill: Permutation

#6 Solution
Answer: C)
$\#Choices_{today} = {}^5P_2$ = 5!/(5 - 2)! = 5 * 4 = 20.
$\#Choices_{tomorrow} = {}^3P_2$ = 3!/1! = 6.
$\#Choices_{day3}$ = 1.
The total number of permutations = 20 * 6 * 1 = 120.
Skill: Permutation

#7 Solution
Answer: C)
This is a combinations problem. The order of the numbers is not relevant.
$^{10}n_5$ = 10!/5!(10 - 5)! = 10 * 9 * 8 * 7 * 6/5 * 4 * 3 * 2 * 1 = 252.
Skill: Combinations

#8 Solution

Answer: E)

There are 3 ways to choose an appetizer, 6 ways to choose a beverage, and 3 ways to choose an entrée. The total number of choices = 3 * 6 * 3 = 54.

Skill: Combinations

#9 Solution

Answer: D)

$^{10}C_3$ = 10!/(3!(10 - 3)!) = 10!/(3! * 7!) = 10 * 9 * 8/3 * 2 * 1 = 120.

Skill: Combinations

#10 Solution

Answer: B)

$^{10}P_4$ = 10!/3!(10 - 3)! = 10 * 9 * 8/3 * 2 * 1 = 120

Skill: Combinations

Section 10: Probabilities, Ratios, Proportions, Rate of Change

1. A class has 50% more boys than girls. What is the ratio of boys to girls?
A) 4:3
B) 3:2
C) 5:4
D) 10:7
E) 7:5

2. A car can travel 30 miles on 4 gallons of gas. If the gas tank has a capacity of 16 gallons, how far can it travel if the tank is ¾ full?
A) 120 miles
B) 90 miles
C) 60 miles
D) 55 miles
E) 65 miles

3. The profits of a company increase by $5000 every year for five years and then decrease by $2000 for the next two years. What is the average rate of change in the company profit for that seven-year period?
A) $1000/yr
B) $2000/yr
C) $3000/yr
D) $4000/yr
E) $5000/yr

4. A bag holds 250 marbles. Of those marbles, 40% are red, 30% are blue, 10% are green, and 20% are black. How many marbles of each color are present in the bag?
A) Red = 90, blue = 80, green = 30, black = 40
B) Red = 80, blue = 60, green = 30, black = 80
C) Red = 100, blue = 75, green = 25, black = 50
D) Red = 100, blue = 70, green = 30, black = 50
E) Red = 120, blue = 100, green = 10, black = 20

5. Two students from a student body of 30 boys and 50 girls will be selected to serve on the school disciplinary committee. What is the probability that first a boy will be chosen, and then a girl?
A) 1/1500
B) 1500/6400
C) 1500/6320
D) 1
E) 30/50

6. If number n, divided by number m, gives a result of .5, what is the relationship between n and m?
A) n is twice as big as m
B) m is three times as big as n
C) n is a negative number
D) m is a negative number
E) n is ½ of m

7. In a fruit basket, there are 10 apples, 5 oranges, 5 pears, and 6 figs. If I select two fruits, what is the probability that I will first pick a pear and then an apple?
A) .07
B) .08
C) 1/13
D) 13
E) 5

8. In a fruit basket, there are 3 apples, 5 oranges, 2 pears, and 2 figs. If I pick out two fruits, what is the probability that I will pick a fig first and then an apple? Round to the nearest 100th.
A) .04
B) .05
C) .06
D) .03
E) .02

9. If x workers can make p toys in c days, how many toys can y workers make in d days if they work at the same rate?
A) cp/qx
B) cq/px
C) cqy/px
D) pdy/cx
E) qy/px

10. If a car travels 35 miles on a gallon of gas, how far will it travel on 13 gallons of gas?
A) 189 miles
B) 255 miles
C) 335 miles
D) 455 miles
E) 500 miles

11. If x workers can do a job in y days, how long will it take x + 5 workers to do the same job?

A) $(x + 5)y$
B) $(x + 5)y^2$
C) $(x^2 - 5)/y$
D) $(x^2 + 5x)/y$
E) $(x^2 + 5)$

12. If 20% of c is equal to 40% of d, what is c/d?

A) 1
B) 2
C) 3
D) 4
E) 5

13. A dealer increased the price of a car by 30%, but then discounted it by 30%. What is the relationship between the final price and the original price?

A) .91x : x
B) .98x : x
C) 1 : 1
D) .88x : x
E) .75x : x

14. If 3/5 of a class of 20 students are girls, what is the ratio of boys to girls?

A) 1:3
B) 2
C) 3
D) 2:3
E) 1

15. Andy can paint a wall in 3 hours. Mike can paint the same wall in 4 hours. How much time will it take them to paint the wall together?

A) 1 hour and 16 minutes.
B) 2 hours.
C) 2 hours and 35 minutes.
D) 1 hour and 42 minutes.
E) Not enough information provided.

16. A bank account has \$35000. The money is split into 14 shares. John gets 2 shares, Mary gets 4 shares, Cindy gets 5 shares, and Jessica gets the rest. How much money does Jessica get?

A) \$10500
B) \$7500
C) \$8000
D) \$4500
E) \$5300

17. A 2400 acre plot of land is split into 5 parts. The first part is 30%, the second part is 5%, the third part is 20%, and the fourth part is 10%. On a pie chart, what angles do each of the divisions represent?

A) 108°, 18°, 72°, 36°, 126°
B) 108°, 20°, 72°, 36^0, 124^0
C) 106°, 20°, 72°, 36°, 126°
D) 30°, 5°, 20°, 10°, 35°
E) 108°, 18°, 72°, 36°, 124°

18. A bag of M&Ms has a total of 30 M&Ms. The bag contains 40% blue M&Ms, 20% red M&Ms, and 10% brown M&Ms. It also contains green M&Ms. What is the probability that two green M&Ms will be picked up in one handful?

A) 81:900
B) 81:870
C) 81:290
D) 24:290
E) 12:150

19. Bag A holds 2 apples and 1 banana. Bag B holds 1 apple and 2 bananas. What is the probability of picking a banana from each bag?

A) 1/3
B) 2/3
C) 1/9
D) 2/9
E) 2

20. Bag A holds 3 apples and 3 bananas. What is the probability of picking two bananas?

A) 1/4
B) 6/20
C) .20
D) 9/30
E) 1/10

Math Section Question Bank: Section 10 – Answers

#1 Solution
Answer: B)
The ratio of boys to girls is 150:100, or 3:2.
Skill: Ratios

#2 Solution
Answer: B)
A full tank has 16 gallons → 3/4 of the tank = 12 gallons. The car can travel 30 miles on 4 gallons, so 12 gallons would take the car 12 * 30/4 = 90 miles.
Skill: Proportions

#3 Solution
Answer: C)
Average Rate of Change = the change in value/change in time = (total profit – initial profit)/change in time. Initial profit = 0, change in time = 7 years.
Increase = 5000 * 5 = 25000; decrease = 2000 * 2 = 4000; total profit = 25000 - 4000 = 21000. (21000 - 0)/7 yrs = $3000/year.
Skill: Rate of Change

#4 Solution
Answer: C)
Total number of marbles = 250.
#red marbles = 250 * 40/100 = 250 * .4 = 100.
#blue marbles = 250 * .3 = 75.
#green marbles = 250 * .1 = 25.
#black marbles = 250 * .2 = 50.
Skill: Ratios

#5 Solution
Answer: C)
The probability of selecting a boy from the entire group = 30:80.
The probability of selecting a girl from the remaining group = 50:79.
The probability of selecting a boy and a girl is (30:80)(50:79) = 1500:6320.
Skill: Probability

#6 Solution
Answer: E)
If n/m = .5, then n = .5m, or n = ½ of m.
Skill: Ratios

#7 Solution

Answer: C)

The total number of fruit = 26.
The probability of picking a pear = 5:26.
The probability of picking an apple = 10:25.
The probability of picking a pear and an apple = 5:26 * 10:25 = 50:650 = 1:13.
Skill: Probability

#8 Solution

Answer: B)

The total number of fruit = 12.
The probability of picking a fig = 2;12.
The probability of picking an apple = 3;11.
The probability of picking a fig and an apple = 2;12 * 3;11 = 6;132 = .045.
Round up to .05.
Skill: Probability

#9 Solution

Answer: D)

The overall rate for x workers = the number of toys/ the number of days, *p/c*. The number of toys one worker makes per day (rate) = *p/cx*. If *q* is the number of toys *y* workers make, and the rates are equal, then the number of toys made = the rate x. The number of days * the number of workers gives us *q* = *p/cx* (*dy*), so:
q = pdy/cx.
Skill: Ratios

#10 Solution

Answer: D)

The distance travelled = (35/1)(13) = 455 miles.
Skill: Ratios

#11 Solution

Answer: D)

It might be tempting to think of this as a direct ratio; where if one increases, the other increases too. However, this is an inverse ratio. x + 5 workers is greater than x workers, so the time required would decrease.
The ratios are inverse → y/x = (x + 5)/n; where n is the number of days.
$n = (x^2 + 5x)/y$.
Skill: Ratios

#12 Solution

Answer: B)

20% of c = 40% of d → .2c = .4d → c:d = 2.
Skill: Ratios

#13 Solution

Answer: A)

Let the original price of the car be x.
After the 30% increase, the price is 1.3x.
After discounting the increased price by 30%, it is now .7 * 1.3x = .91x.
The ratio of the final price to the original price = .91x : x.
Skill: Percentages and Ratios

#14 Solution

Answer: D)

If 3/5 of the class is girls, then 2/5 is boys.
The ratio of boys to girls = 2:3.
Skill: Ratios

#15 Solution

Answer: D)

If Andy paints 1 wall in 3 hours, he will only be able to paint 1/3 of the wall in 1 hour. If Mike paints 1 wall in 4 hours, he will only be able to paint 1/4 of the wall in 1 hour. If Mike and Andy work together to paint the wall for 1 hour, they will paint 1/3 + 1/4 of the wall, or 7/12 of the wall.
If x is the total number of hours needed for them to finish painting the wall, then (7/12) * x = 1.
x = 12/7 = 1.71, round to 1.7.
1.7 hours = 1 hour + .7 hour = 1 hour + .7 * 60 minutes = 1 hour and 42 minutes.
Skill: Proportions

#16 Solution

Answer: B)

Total number of shares = 14. Therefore Jessica's part is 14 - (2 + 4 + 5) = 3.
So Jessica's share of the inheritance = 3/14 * 35000 = 7500.
Skill: Proportions

#17 Solution

Answer: A)

The angle around the center of a circle = 360°.
The part that is 30% subtends an angle of 30/100 * 360 = 108°.
The part that is 5% subtends an angle of 5/100 * 360 = 18°.
The part that is 20% subtends an angle of 20/100 * 360 = 72°.
The part that is 10% subtends an angle of 10/100 * 360 = 36°.
The remaining part that is 35% subtends an angle of 35/100 * 360 = 126°.
Skill: Proportions

#18 Solution
Answer: D)
First find the portion of each color.
Blue: .4 * 30 = 12.
Red: .2 * 30 = 6.
Brown: .1 * 30 = 3.
Green: 9.
The probability of picking two green M&Ms in one handful:
9/30 * 8/29 = 3/10 * 8/29 = 24/290.
Skill: Probability

#19 Solution
Answer: D)
$Prob_{Bag\ A}$ = 1/3.
$Prob_{Bag\ B}$ = 2/3.
The total probability = (1/3)(2/3), which is 2/9.
Skill: Probability

#20 Solution
Answer: C)
$Prob_1$ = 3/6.
$Prob_2$ = 2/5.
The total probability = (3/6)(2/5) = 6/30 = 1/5 = .20.
Skill: Probability

Section 11: Trigonometry and Plane Geometry

Questions 1-3 use the right triangle ABC below.

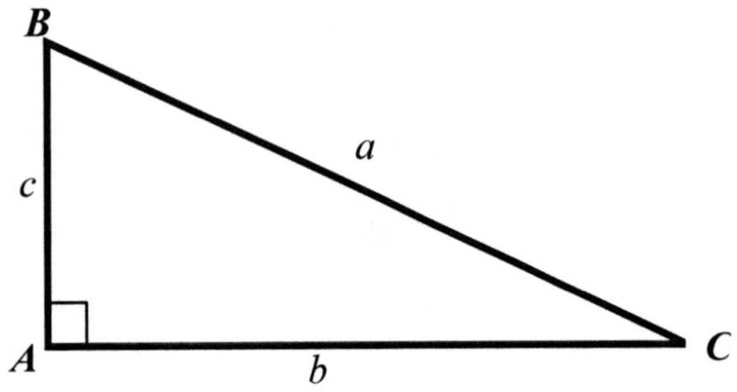

1. What is cos C?
A) c/a
B) c/b
C) 1
D) 0
E) b/a

2. If the value of angle B is 45°, which of the following must be the ratio of line segments c:a?
A) 1:1
B) 1:2
C) $1:\sqrt{3/2}$
D) $1:\sqrt{2}$
E) Cannot be determined from the information given.

3. If the value of angle C is 45°, and line segment *c* has length 4, what is the closest approximation of the length of line segment *a*?

A) $\sqrt{3/2}$
B) 5.7
C) 5
D) 3
E) Cannot be determined from the information given.

4. Which of the following graphs best approximates the function y = 3(sin(x))?

A) 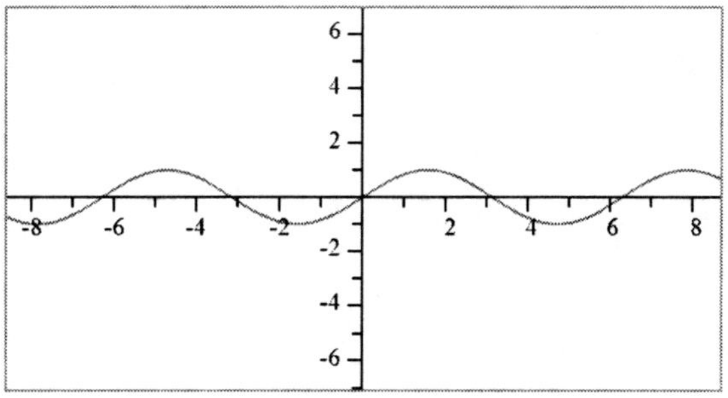

B) 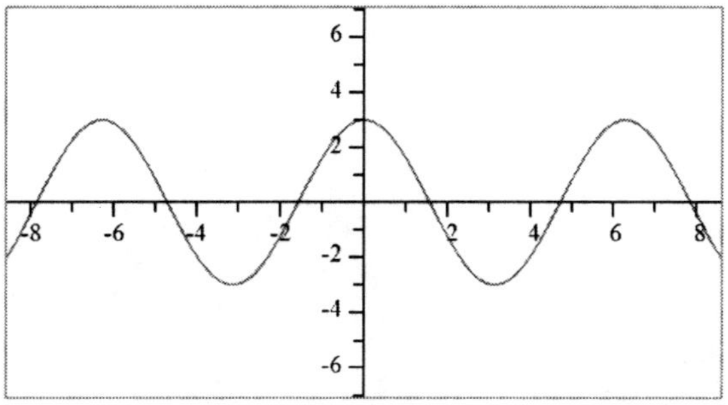

C) 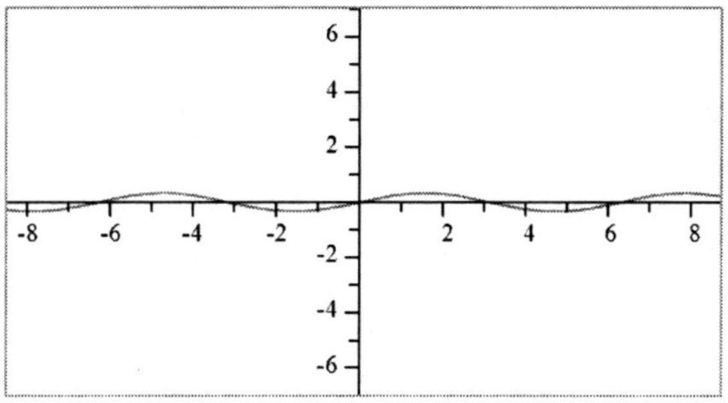

D) 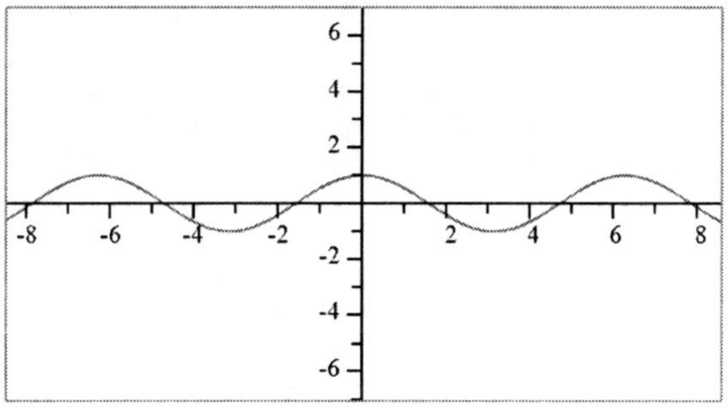

E) 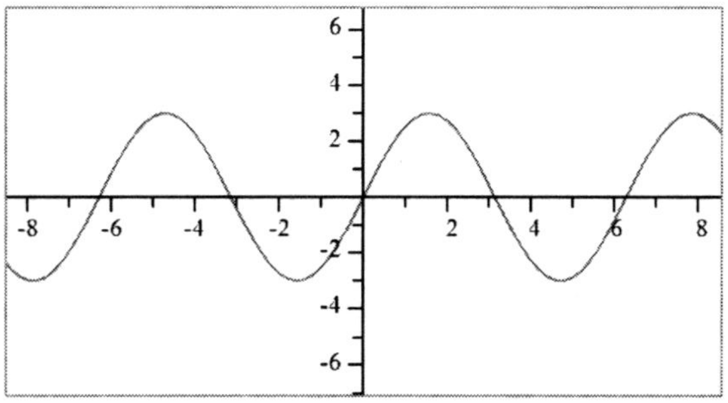

5. Which of the following is equivalent to 1 for any angle Θ?

A) $\sin^2\Theta + \cos^2\Theta$

B) $1/(\sin^2\Theta + \tan^2\Theta)$

C) $\csc^2\Theta + \sec^2\Theta$

D) $\sin\Theta/\tan\Theta$

E) $\cos\Theta$

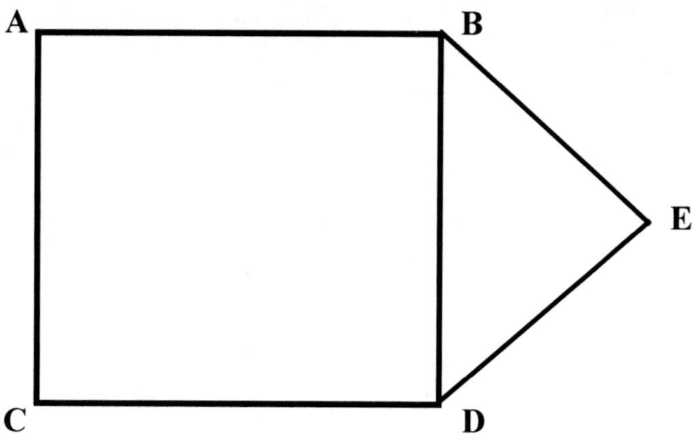

Questions 6-9 use the diagram above. ABCD is a square with sides of length 2.5. Angle DBE is 28°, and angle BED is a right angle.

6. What is the area of ABCD?
A) 7.5
B) 10
C) 6.25
D) 4.25
E) 12.5

7. What is the approximate length of segment DE?
A) 1.2
B) 2.2
C) 1.7
D) 2.5
E) 0.2

8. What is the approximate perimeter of polygon ABEDC?
A) 10
B) 10.5
C) 8.7
D) 10.9
E) 12.2

9. What is the measure of angle EDB, in degrees?
A) 82
B) 62
C) 90
D) 28
E) 115

Questions 10-12 use the below information:

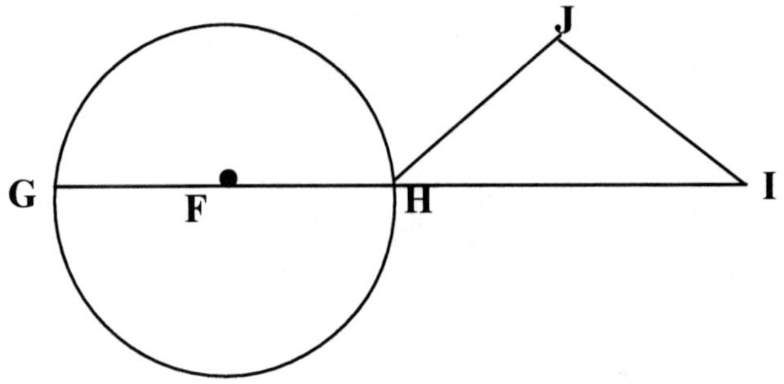

Point H lies in the middle of line GI. Triangle HIJ is an isosceles triangle, with segments HJ and IJ being equal. The length of GI is 7. Point F is the center of the circle. Angle JHI is 25°.

10. The circumference of the circle above is:

A) 3.5π
B) 7π
C) 7
D) 12.5
E) 14π

11. What is the value in degrees of angle HJI?

A) 25°
B) 50°
C) 110°
D) 130°
E) It cannot be determined from the information given.

12. What is the area of the two shapes above line GI (the triangle and the circle segment)?

A) $\pi(1.75^2) + (0.5)(3.5)(1.75)\cos(25)$
B) $(0.5)[\,\pi(3.5^2) + (3.5)(1.75)\cos(25)]$
C) $[\,\pi(1.75^2) + (3.5)(1.75)\tan(25)]/2$
D) $[\,\pi(1.75^2) + (3.5)(1.75)\tan(25)]$
E) $(0.5)[\,\pi(3.5^2) + (3.5)(1.75)\sin(25)]$

13. What is the degree measure of the smaller angle formed by the hands of a circular wall clock that reads 2:00?

A) 12°
B) 30°
C) 45°
D) 50°
E) 60°

Questions 14-15 use the right triangle below:

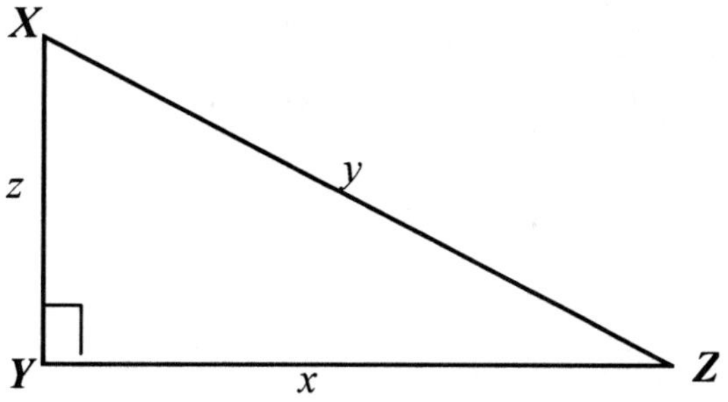

14. Which of the following equivalencies is true?
A) (sin(X))/x = (sin(Y)/y
B) tan(Z) = x/z
C) sin(X) = (sec(X))/1
D) z + x = (sin(X) + sin(Z))/y
E) tan(Y)=1

15. If X=50°, then what is the length of line segment x?:
A) 4
B) 4.5
C) 3.8
D) 5.0
E) Cannot be determined from the information given.

16. An angle Θ is formed between the line segment extending five units from the origin of a coordinate plane and the positive x axis. If cosΘ = -0.8, in which quadrant of the coordinate plane does the line segment fall?
A) I
B) II
C) III
D) IV
E) Cannot be determined from the information given

17. A building is 5 stories tall, and each story is 12 feet high. At a certain time in the day, the building casts a shadow that is 80 feet long from the base of the building. Approximately what angle do the sun's rays hit the building at that time of day?
A) 80°
B) 65°
C) 58°
D) 53°
E) 40°

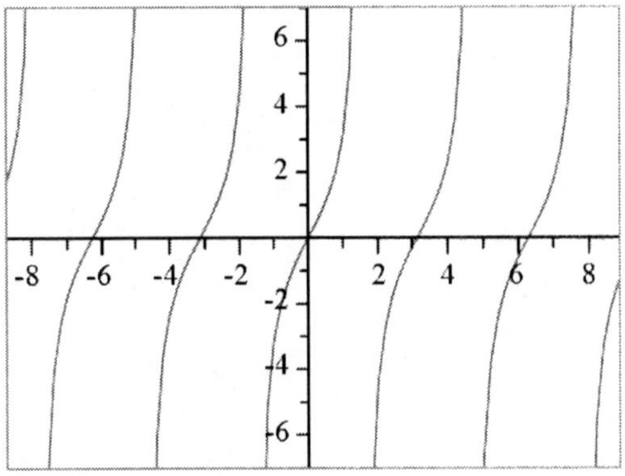

18. The graph above represents which of the following equations?

A) y=2sin(x)
B) y=tan(x)/2
C) y=csc(x)
D) y=2tan(x)
E) y=sin(x)/cos(x)

Questions 19 and 20 use the following information:
A yard forms a right triangle. The longest edge of the yard, which borders a field, is 18 meters. The edge bordering the house is 12 meters long. The last edge borders a neighbor's yard.

19. What is the approximate measure of the angle, in degrees, between the field and the neighbor's yard?

A) 90°
B) 55°
C) 48°
D) 42°
E) 32°

20. The neighbors wish to construct a fence between the two yards. Approximately how many meters of fencing material will be needed to build the fence?

A) 12.0
B) 13.0
C) 13.4
D) 15.2
E) 18.0

Math Section Question Bank: Section 11 – Answers

#1 Solution
Answer: E)
The cosine of an angle is the adjacent segment divided by the hypotenuse.
(Cos(angle C) = segment b/segment a)
Skill: Trigonometry

#2 Solution
Answer: D)
sin (45) = $\sqrt{2}$
It is a common trig identity that triangles with angles of 45, 45, and 90 degrees have sides of ratio 1:1: $\sqrt{2}$.
Skill: Trigonometry

#3 Solution
Answer: B)
4/sin(45)=5.65
Skill: Trigonometry

#4 Solution
Answer: E)
Stretching trigonometric graphs. Graph E shows the sine wave amplified by the coefficient 3.
Skill: Graphing Trigonometric Functions

#5 Solution
Answer: A)
Basic trigonometry definition.
Skill: Trigonometry

#6 Solution
Answer: C)
Simply find the area of a square.
2.5 * 2.5 = 6.25
Skill: Geometry

#7 Solution
Answer: A)
Because BED is a right triangle, with BD, of length 2.5, as the hypotenuse, we can use: sin(28)=DE/2.5
Skill: Geometry and Trigonometry

#8 Solution

Answer: D)

To find the perimeter, we sum all of the segments except for BD. BE and ED are found using trig equations.

2.5 + 2.5 + 2.5 + 1.2 + 2.2 = 10.9

Skill: Geometry and Trigonometry

#9 Solution

Answer: B)

Because we know the other two angles in the triangle to be 90 and 28 degrees, we can find the third by subtracting those from 180:180-(90+28)=62

Skill: Geometry

#10 Solution

Answer: A)

The radius is one-fourth of segment GI, and the circumference equals the radius times 2π.

$C=2\pi r$ $C=2\pi(7/4)$

Skill: Geometry

#11 Solution

Answer: D)

Since the triangle is isosceles, 180 - 2(25) gives the angle measure.

Skill: Geometry and Trigonometry

#12 Solution

Answer: C)

The formula for the area of a circle divided by 2, because we only need half of the circle, plus the formula for the area of the triangle, incorporating trig to find the height of the triangle:

$\pi/2(1.75^2) + (1/2)(3.5)(1.75)\tan(25)$

Skill: Geometry

#13 Solution

Answer: E)

A clock has twelve segments, and the angle formed by the hands at 2:00 will include two of those segments. Therefore we can use a proportion:(2/12)=(x/360)

Skill: Trigonometry

#14 Solution

Answer: A)

This equivalency is true for any triangle. If you do not have this memorized, you can still arrive at it by eliminating the other answer choices.

Skill: Trigonometry

#15 Solution

Answer: E)

Any of the other lengths is needed to solve this problem.

Skill: Trigonometry

#16 Solution

Answer: B)

The angle is around 145°, placing the line segment in the second quadrant.

$\cos^{-1}(-.08)=143.13$

Skill: Trigonometry and Coordinate Geometry

#17 Solution

Answer: D)

The building and shadow form a right triangle of height 60 and base 80.

$\text{Tan}(x) = 80/60$.

Skill: Trigonometry

#18 Solution

Answer: D)

This is a graph of tan(x), which you should recognize. However, the graph has been stretched, so it is D rather than B.

Skill: Trigonometry

#19 Solution

Answer: D)

The yard makes a right triangle with a hypotenuse of length 18 and one side of length 12. To find the angle between the hypotenuse and the third side, use equation:

$\sin(x) = (12/18)$

Skill: Trigonometry and Geometry

#20 Solution

Answer: C)

This question is asking for the length of the third side of the yard, which is not given. Use the Pythagorean Theorem to find the length:

$x^2 + 12^2 = 18^2$

Skill: Geometry

Chapter 11: English Section Question Bank

Directions:

This test consists of four passages. In each passage, certain words and phrases have been underlined and numbered. The questions on each passage consist of alternatives for these underlined segments. Choose the alternative that follows standard written English, most accurately reflects the style and tone of the passage, or best relays the idea of the passage. Choose "No Change" if no change is necessary.

You are to choose the best answer to the question.

You will also find questions about a section of the passage, or the passage as a whole. These questions do not refer to the underlined portions of the passage, but are identified by a boxed number. For each question, choose the alternative that best answers the question.

PASSAGE I

Examining my Ecological Footprint

<u>Examining the impact my lifestyle has on the earth's resources is, I believe, a fascinating and valuable thing to do</u>.[1] According to the Earth Day Network ecological footprint calculator created by the Sierra Club, it would take four planet earths to sustain the human population if everyone used as many resources as I do. <u>My</u>[2] "ecological footprint," or the amount of productive area of the earth that is required to produce the resources I consume, <u>must then be much</u>[2] larger <u>than the footprints of</u>[3] most of the population. It is hard to balance the luxuries and opportunities I

1.
A) NO CHANGE
B) Examining the impact my lifestyle has on the earth's resources is a fascinating and valuable thing to do.
C) The impact of my lifestyle on the earth's resources is fascinating and valuable to examine.
D). It is fascinating and valuable to examine the impact my lifestyle has on the earth's resources.

2.
F) NO CHANGE
G) Making my…, much
H) The…, must then be much
J) The…, much

3.
A) NO CHANGE
B) than those
C) than footprints of
D) as the footprints of

have available to me with doing what I know to be better from an ecological standpoint.
4

One's ecological footprint is measured with accounting for different factors such as how often and how far one drives and travels by air, what kind of structure one lives in, and what kind of goods one consumes (and how far those consumer goods travel across the globe). For example, a person who lives in a freestanding home, which uses more energy to heat and cool than an apartment in a building would;
5

who travels internationally several times per year; and who eats exotic, out-of-season foods which must be shipped in from other countries, rather than locally grown and raised food which is in season, would have a large ecological footprint.
6

[7]

Although I get points for my recycling habits, my use of public transportation, and living in an apartment complex rather than a free-standing residence; my footprint expands when it is taken into account my not-entirely-local diet, my occasional use of a car, my three magazine
8

4.
F) NO CHANGE
G) me, with
H) me; with
J) me: with

5.
A) NO CHANGE
B) measured by
C) measuring with
D) measured of

6.
F) NO CHANGE
G) that is
H) that are
J) which are

7.
Both sentences in the above paragraph are examples of:

A) Run-on sentences.
B) Redundancy.
C) Loaded sentences.
D) Circumlocution.

8.
F) NO CHANGE
G) use of
H) using
J) my using

subscriptions, and my history of flying more than ten hours a year. These are all examples of things that use a large amount of resources.

9

9.

The writer is editing the above paragraph, the whole of which is two sentences. Which of the following would be the best choice for improvement?

A) NO CHANGE
B) Divide the first sentence into two sentences and delete the second sentence.
C) Combine the information in both Sentences, then divide it into three shorter sentences.
D) Divide the first sentence into two sentences and keep the second sentence as is.

This examination of the impact my lifestyle has on the earth's resources
10
is fascinating and valuable to me. It is fairly easy for me to recycle, so I do it,

10.

F) NO CHANGE
G) on the resources of the planet
H) had on the earth's resources
J) has on the earth resources

but it would be much harder to forgoing
11
the opportunity to travel by plane or eat my favorite

11.

A) NO CHANGE
B) forgo
C) have forgone
D) not forgo

fruits; that
12
have been flown to the supermarket from a different country. I feel that realizing just how

12.

F) NO CHANGE
G) fruits, that
H) fruits that
J) fruits: that

unfair my share of the earths' resources has
13
been should help me to change at least some of my bad habit. Perhaps if we were all made aware of the true

13.

A) NO CHANGE
B) earth's resources has
C) earths' resources have
D) earth's resources have

cost of our habits, actions, and choices, people [14] would be more likely to take steps to reduce his or her [15] consumption of the earth's resources.

14.
F) NO CHANGE
G) choices. People
H) choices; people
J) then people

15.
A) NO CHANGE
B) our
C) their
D) one's

PASSAGE II
The Sculptor Augusta Savage

Augusta Savage: were [16] a world-famous African-American sculptor. Born in Florida, [17] her first formal art training was in New York City at Cooper Union, the school recommended to her by Solon Gorglum. While she studied, [18] she supported herself by doing odd jobs, including clerking and working in laundries. In 1926 she exhibited her work at the Sesquicentennial Exposition in Philadelphia. That same year she was awarded a scholarship to study in Rome. However, she was unable to accept the award because she could not raise the money she would have needed [19] to live there.

16.
F) NO CHANGE
G) Savage, was
H) Savage, were
J) Savage was

17.
A) NO CHANGE
B) She was born in Florida,
C) Although born in Florida,
D) DELETE

18.
F) NO CHANGE
G) While she studied
H) Move segment to the end of the sentence.
J) DELETE

19.
A) NO CHANGE
B) she would need
C) she needed
D) she needs

When she returned to the United States, she exhibited her work at several important galleries. <u>In addition to her own work,</u> [20.] Augusta Savage taught art classes in Harlem. During the Depression, she helped African- American artists to enroll in the Works Progress Administration arts project. Throughout her career, she was an active spokesperson for African-American artists in the United <u>States. She</u> [21] also was one of the principal organizers of the Harlem Artists Guild.

20.
F) NO CHANGE
G) Additional to creating her own work,
H) Additionally to her own work,
J) In addition to creating her own work,

21.
A) NO CHANGE
B) States; she
C) States, she
D) States and she

In <u>1923, Savage</u> [22] applied for a summer art program sponsored by the French government; despite being more than qualified, she was turned down by the international judging committee, solely because of her race. Savage was deeply <u>upset, questioning</u> [23] the committee, beginning the first of many public fights for equal rights in her life. The incident got press coverage on both sides of the Atlantic, and eventually the sole supportive committee member, sculptor Hermon Atkins MacNeil—who at one time had shared a studio with Henry Ossawa Tanner—<u>invited her to study with him</u> [24].

22.
F) NO CHANGE
G) 1923 Savage
H) 1923 Savage,
J) 1923; Savage

23.
A) NO CHANGE
B) upset and questioning
C) upset, and questioning
D) upset, and so she questioned

24.
F) NO CHANGE
G) invited her to study with himself
H) had invited her to study with him
J) gave her an invitation to study with him

She later <u>sited</u> him as one of her teachers.
25

In 1939, Augusta Savage received a commission from the World's Fair and created a 16 foot tall plaster sculpture called *Lift Ev'ry Voice and Sing*. Savage did not have any funds for a bronze cast, or even to move and store <u>it</u>, and it was
26
destroyed by bulldozers at the close of the fair. However, small metal and plaster souvenir copies of the sculpture <u>has</u> survived.
27

28

Perhaps Savage's more indelible legacy is the work of the students whom she taught in her studio, the Savage Studio of Arts and Crafts. Her students included Jacob Lawrence, Norman Lewis, and Gwendolyn Knight. Lawrence was a Cubist painter whose work is hosted in museums across the country. Lewis was an Abstract Expressionist painter who often dealt with music and jazz in abstract ways. <u>Knight who was born in Barbados</u>
29
founded an organization to support young artists.

25.
A) NO CHANGE
B) siting
C) would site
D) cite

26.
F) NO CHANGE
G) the statue
H) them
J) her

27.
A) NO CHANGE
B) have
C) were
D) would

28.
Which sentence would best fit at the beginning of the above paragraph?
F) Her education in the arts was substantial after working with so many high profile sculptors.
G) African-Americans were still facing terrible discrimination at the end of the 1930's.
H) The World's Fair is a hug art exhibit that occurs every two to four years.
J) Throughout the 1930's, her Profile as an artist continued to grow.

29.
A) NO CHANGE
B) Knight, who was born in Barbados
C) Knight who was born in Barbados,
D) Knight, who was born in Barbados,

Augusta Savage <u>worked tireless</u> [30] to teach these artists, help them to secure funding, and support their careers.

30.

F) NO CHANGE
G) worked tirelessly
H) worked herself tireless
J) was working tireless

PASSAGE III
History of Art for Beginners and Students – Ancient Painting

The following passage is adapted from Clara Erskine Clément's <u>History of Art for Beginners and Students</u>, first published in 1887 (public domain; errors inserted for the purposes of crafting questions).

In speaking of art we often contrast the useful or mechanical arts with the Fine <u>Arts; by</u> [31] these terms we denote the difference between the arts which are used in making such things as are necessary and useful in civilized life, and the arts by which ornamental and beautiful things are made. The fine arts are Architecture, Sculpture, Painting, Poetry, and Music, and though we could live if none of these <u>existed, yet</u> [32] life would be far from the pleasant experience that it is often <u>made to be</u> [33] through the enjoyment of these arts.

31.

A) NO CHANGE
B) Arts, by
C) Arts. By
D) Arts by

32.

F) NO CHANGE
G) existed,
H) yet,
J) existed and yet

33.

A) NO CHANGE
B) made out to be
C) made
D) is

In speaking of Painting, just here I wish to include the more general idea of pictures of various sorts, and it seems to me that while picture-making belongs to the fine or beautiful arts, it is now made a very useful art in many ways. For example, when a school-book is illustrated, how much more easily we understand the subject we are studying through the help we get from pictures of objects or places that we have not seen, and yet wish to know about. Pictures of natural scenery bring all countries before our eyes in such a way that by looking at it, while **34** reading books of travel, we may know a great deal more about lands we have never seen, and may never be able to visit.

34.

F) NO CHANGE
G) those
H) them
J) one

35

35.

Which of the following sentences could be added to the above paragraph to further the point being made?

A) Pictures are not useful, however, when they distract students from the purpose of a text.
B) Pictures can be a beautiful Addition to a living space.
C) Doctors often use pictures when studying the body to help them learn organs and systems.
D) People really don't travel to other lands anymore.

St. Augustine, who wrote in the fourth century, says **36** that "pictures are the books of the simple or unlearned;" this is just as true now as then, and we should regard pictures as one of the most agreeable means of education. The cultivation of the imagination is very important because in **37** this way we can add much to our individual happiness. Thus one of the uses of pictures is that they give us a

36.

F) NO CHANGE
G) century says
H) century said
J) century, said

37.

A) NO CHANGE
B) important, because in
C) important; because in
D) important; in

clear idea of what we have not seen; a second use is that they <u>are exciting to</u> **38** our imaginations, and often help us to forget disagreeable circumstances and unpleasant surroundings. Through this power, if we are in a dark, narrow street, in a house which is not to our liking, <u>or in the midst of any unpleasant happenings</u> **39**, we are able to fix our thoughts upon a photograph or picture that may be there, and by studying it we are able to imagine ourselves far, far away, in some spot where nature makes everything pleasant and soothes us into forgetfulness of all that can disturb our happiness. Many an invalid—many an unfortunate one is thus made content by pictures during hours that would <u>otherwise</u> **40** be wretched. This is the result of cultivating the perceptive and imaginative <u>faculties, and when</u> **41** this is done, we have a source of pleasure within ourselves and not dependent on others which can never be taken from us.

It often happens that we see two persons <u>doing</u> **42** the same work and are situated in the same way in the world who are very different in their <u>manner one</u> **43** is light-hearted and happy, the other heavy and sad. If you can find out the truth, it will result that the sad one is matter-of-fact, and has no

38.

F) NO CHANGE
G) exciting
H) excite
J) excited

39.

If the writer deletes this section of the sentence, what will be lost?

A) NO CHANGE
B) The argument that pictures are useful.
C) The example of pictures being educational.
D) The generalization of the example.

40.

F) NO CHANGE
G) other wise
H) however
J) DELETE

41.

A) NO CHANGE
B) faculties and when
C) faculties, and, when
D) faculties; when

42.

F) NO CHANGE
G) are doing
H) who do
J) done

43.

A) NO CHANGE
B) manner; one
C) manner. One
D) manner: one

imagination—he can only think of his work and what <u>concerns</u> **44** him personally; but the merry one would surprise you if you could read his thoughts—if you could know the distances they have passed over, and what a vast difference there is between his thought and his work. So while it is natural for almost every one to exclaim <u>joyful</u> **45** at the beauty of pictures, and to enjoy looking at them simply, I wish my readers to think of their uses also, and understand the benefits that may be derived from them. I have only hinted at a few of these uses, but many others will occur to you.

44.

F) NO CHANGE
G) troubles
H) is about
J) it means to

45.

A) NO CHANGE
B) joyfully
C) joy
D) with joy

PASSAGE IV
Air Travel, Then and Now

Traveling on commercial airlines has changed substantially over years[46]. When commercial air travel first became available, it was so expensive that usually only businessmen could afford to do so[47]. Airplane efficiency, the relative cost of fossil fuels, and using economies[48] of scale have all contributed to make travel by air more affordable and common. These days, there are nearly 30,000 commercial air flights in the world each day!

Depending on the size of the airport you are departing from, you should arrive 90 minutes to[49] two and a half hours before your plane leaves. Things like checking your luggage and flying internationally can make the process of getting to your gate take longer. If you fly out of a very busy airport, like LaGuardia, in[50] New York City, on a very busy travel day, like the day before Thanksgiving, you can easily miss your flight if you don't arrive early enough.

Security processes for passengers have also changed. In the 1960s, there was hardly any[51] security: you could just buy your ticket and walk on to the plane the day of the flight without even

46.
F) NO CHANGE
G) over the years
H) over time
J) DELETE

47.
A) NO CHANGE
B) to do it
C) to fly
D) do so

48.
F) NO CHANGE
G) using economies
H) and the use of economies
J) and economies

49.
A) NO CHANGE
B) one and a half hours to
C) an hour and a half to
D) up to

50.
F) NO CHANGE
G) La Guardia in
H) La Guardia; in
J) La Guardia,

51.
A) NO CHANGE
B) hardly
C) no
D) barely

needing to show identification. In the 1970s, American commercial airlines started installing sky marshals on many flights, an [52] undercover law enforcement officers who would protect the passengers from a potential hijacking.

Also in the early 1970s, the federal government began to require that airlines screen passengers and their luggage for things like weapons and bombs. After the 2001 terrorist attacks in the United States, these requirements were stringently enforced [53]. Family members can no longer meet someone at the gate; only ticketed passengers are allowed into the gate area [54].

The definition of weapons are [55] not allowed is expanded every time there is a new incident for example [56] liquids are now restricted on planes after an attempted planned attack using gel explosives in 2006.

52.

F) NO CHANGE
G) flights; an
H) flights. Marshals are
J) flights, marshals are

53.

A) NO CHANGE
B) stiffly upheld
C) enforced with more stringency
D) more stringently enforced

54.

If this section was deleted the passage would lose:

F) NO CHANGE
G) An explanation of the screening process.
H) Ambiguity over why family members are no longer allowed at the gate.
J) A further specific example of how regulations have changed over time.

55.

A) NO CHANGE
B) weapon is
C) weapons
D) weapons which are

56.

F) NO CHANGE
G) incident, for example,
H) incident; for example
J) incident. For example,

Despite the hassles of traveling by air, it is still a boon to modern life. Still, some businesses are moving away from sending employees on airplane trips, as face-to-face video conferencing technologies improve. A trip which might take ten hours by car can take only two hours by plane. However, the ability to travel quickly by air will always be valued, by citizens of our modern society.

(Underlined portions: 57 "life. Still, some"; 58 "as"; 59 "can take only"; 60 "will always be valued, by citizens")

57.

A) NO CHANGE
B) life. Some
C) life even though some
D) life, still some

58.

F) NO CHANGE
G) because
H) while
J) since

59.

A) NO CHANGE
B) may only take
C) takes only
D) will only take

60.

F) NO CHANGE
G) citizens will always value
H) will always, be valued by citizens
J) will always be valued by citizens

English Section Question Bank – Answers

1.	D)	16.	J)	31.	C)	46.	G)
2.	F)	17.	C)	32.	G)	47.	C)
3.	A)	18.	H)	33.	A)	48.	J)
4.	F)	19.	A)	34.	H)	49.	B)
5.	B)	20.	J)	35.	C)	50.	G)
6.	F)	21.	A)	36.	J)	51.	A)
7.	D)	22.	F)	37.	B)	52.	H)
8.	G)	23.	D)	38.	H)	53.	D)
9.	C)	24.	F)	39.	D)	54.	J)
10.	F)	25.	D)	40.	F)	55.	D)
11.	B)	26.	G)	41.	A)	56.	J)
12.	H)	27.	B)	42.	H)	57.	C)
13.	B)	28.	J)	43.	B)	58.	F)
14.	F)	29.	D)	44.	F)	59.	B)
15.	C)	30.	G)	45.	B)	60.	J)

Chapter 12: Writing Section Question Bank

Sample Essay Prompt 1:

Some schools are now requiring graduating seniors to complete an independent project. These projects can take many forms: exploring a unique research inquiry; organizing a community event; or writing, performing, or recording an original work. Supporters believe this requirement can prompt students to learn how to manage their time, work with a faculty advisor, organize a large-scale project, and explore an interest. However, some educators feel that the strain of an open-ended project would be too stressful for seniors, who already have many obligations. In your opinion, should high school seniors be required to complete an independent project?

In your essay, take a position on this question. You may write about either one of the two points of view given, or you may present a different point of view on this question. Use specific reasons and examples to support your position.

Sample Essay Prompt 2:

These days, most people have some presence on a social networking site: Facebook, Twitter, LinkedIn, etc. Employers have begun screening job candidates using these different social networking sites, with some employers going so far as to require applicants to grant them full access to their social media profiles. This is viewed by some as an invasion of privacy, but others feel that when the job market is tight, job applicants should be prepared to have all aspects of their lives scrutinized in the application process. In your opinion, should employers be allowed to ask applicants for full access to social media profiles?

In your essay, take a position on this question. You may write about either one of the two points of view given, or you may present a different point of view on this question. Use specific reasons and examples to support your position.

Sample Essay Prompt 3:

In the past, college admissions boards have generally frowned upon students who take a "gap year" between high school and college to work, travel, or volunteer. It was thought that students who did this were not serious about learning and would be unsuccessful at college. However, ideas of what constitutes a successful academic path are changing; and now some college admission boards are favoring students who take this gap year, viewing it as an enriching and maturing experience. In your opinion, should high school graduates who plan to attend college delay their freshman year?

In your essay, take a position on this question. You may write about either one of the two points of view given, or you may present a different point of view on this question. Use specific reasons and examples to support your position.

Writing Section Question Bank – Answers

Essay Prompt 1

Essay Prompt 1: High Scoring Essay (Score of 10 – 12)

High school seniors face myriad obligations: completing the most advanced courses they've ever taken, applying to colleges and deciding what to do with their lives the next year, perhaps working a job to save money for college, and certainly spending time with their good friends whom they may not get to see much after high school. Despite these heavy burdens, I think that adding an independent senior project to the load would help senior students immensely. Doing a senior project will help students clarify their skills and interests and will ultimately help them decide where to go for college and what to study, and will help them to be successful when they arrive.

Many of the classes that students take in high school are required by the state curriculums, and do not necessarily offer students the chance to explore their interests. As a result, students might wait until college to pursue something that they think will interest them, whether it is artistic, like photography, or more technical, like engineering. A student might take these more specialized classes for a year, spending considerable time and money exploring something that they might ultimately decide is not a good fit for them. Giving students the chance to explore a specialized interest in a structured way during high school can afford students a less expensive way to try on a new interest. A year of independent study along an interesting topic, whether it be photographing landscapes or designing bridges or anything in between, can take a student to new and unexpected topics and passions. He or she can then begin college with a much clearer idea of what to study, and will spend less time taking general studies classes or pursuing a misguided degree plan.

In addition to helping students decide what they are passionate about, this type of project will provide students with skills that will be critical to success in college. High school is great for preparing students to absorb the more difficult concepts in college, but falls short in preparing students for the habits and self-motivation they will need. An open-ended senior project will give students a taste of how they need to manage their time to accomplish large, open-ended goals over a long period of time. Another skill this type of project could help students develop is how to work with an advisor. Students will need a faculty advisor to help them manage a project of this magnitude, and that will teach students how to prepare for meetings, how to ask for feedback, and respect an advisor's time. These skills are usually only learned the hard way, and it would be better for students to learn that in high school so that they can make the most of their critical advising relationships in college.

The purpose of an independent senior project for high school students would be the same as the purpose of high school itself: to prepare students for attending college, working successfully at jobs, and being productive members of society. However by its nature, it might be better at accomplishing those aims than anything else a student does in their last year at school. Students should be given this fantastic opportunity to explore their interests and learn the valuable lessons that come from independent and large-scale thinking.

Essay Prompt 1: Medium Scoring Essay (Score of 7 – 9)

High school seniors face a lot of obligations: completing the most advanced courses they've ever taken, applying to colleges and deciding what to do with their lives the next year, perhaps working a job to save money for college, and certainly spending time with their good friends whom they may not get to see much after high school. However I think that adding an independent senior project to the load would help senior students immensely. Doing a senior project will help students clarify their skills and interests and will ultimately help them decide where to go for college and what to study, and will help them to be successful when they arrive.

Many of the classes that students take in high school are required by the state curriculums, and do not necessarily offer students the chance to explore their interests. As a result, students might wait until college to pursue something that they think will interest them, whether it is artistic, like photography, or more technical, like engineering. Giving students the chance to explore their real interests during high school can afford students a way to try on a new interest. A year of independent study along an interesting topic, can take a student to new and unexpected topics and passions. They she can then begin college with a better idea of what to study, and will spend less time taking general studies classes or pursuing the wrong degree plan.

Also this type of project will provide students with skills that will be critical to success in college. High school is great for preparing students to absorb the more difficult concepts in college, but falls short in preparing students for the habits and self-motivation they will need. An open-ended senior project will give students a taste of how they need to manage their time to accomplish large, open-ended goals over a long period of time.

The purpose of an independent senior project for high school students would be the same as the purpose of high school itself: to prepare students for attending college, working successfully at jobs, and being productive members of society. It might even be better at accomplishing those aims than anything else a student does in their last year at school. Students should be given this fantastic opportunity to explore their interests and learn the valuable lessons that come from independent and large-scale thinking.

Essay Prompt 1: Low Scoring Essay (Score of 2 – 6)

I think that adding an independent senior project to the load would help senior students immensely. Doing a senior project will help students clarify their skills and interests and will ultimately help them decide where to go for college and what to study. Many of the classes that students take in high school are required, and do not give students the chance to explore their interests. As a result, students might wait until college to pursue something that they think will interest them. Giving students the chance to explore their real interests during high school can afford students a way to try on a new interest. A year of independent study along an interesting topic, can take a student to new and unexpected topics and passions. They she can then begin college with a better idea of what to study, and will spend less time taking general studies classes or pursuing the wrong degree plan.

The purpose of an independent senior project for high school students would be the same as the purpose of high school itself: to prepare students for attending college, working successfully at jobs, and being productive members of society. It might even be better at accomplishing those aims than anything else a student does in their last year at school. Students should be given this chance to explore their interests and learn valuable lessons.

Essay Prompt 2

Essay Prompt 2: High Scoring Essay (Score of 10 – 12)

It is understandable that some employers are making the mistake of asking potential employees for the passwords to their personal social media accounts. Companies are anxious to view the social media profiles of their prospective hires because hiring is a risk for companies to take. Employers fear hiring an employee who will turn out to be volatile or unreliable. They also want to hire those who will fit into the culture of their company and who will make the company look good. However, snooping into personal social media profiles is not the way to accomplish this for several reasons: private information is not relevant to the way a person acts professionally, it opens the door for discrimination, and it sets a dangerous precedent for privacy rights.

There is a generational gap in how social media is viewed and used. For students of this generation, a social media website, for example Facebook, serves as much more than just a way to show information to the world. Students today use Facebook for email and messaging, private applications which have no bearing on public image. An employer asking a teenager for user access to her Facebook profile might just ask well ask for the passwords to her personal email account and her voicemail as well. It is simply an invasion of privacy on a scale that is not acceptable in today's marketplace. No one, potential employers included, are allowed to open someone's mail in their mailbox; the digital equivalent of that is just relevant, if not more relevant (most of us receive way more sensitive information via Facebook messaging than via snail mail these days), and should be just as protected.

Employers can still do what anyone else can do – perform a Google search on a person. Through that, they can view all the information about a person which is public. Since that is the information that potential customers of a company can see about the employees, then that should be perfectly sufficient in screening applicants. If an applicant has a Facebook profile which is made public and full of obscenities, slurs, and references to getting wasted, then the employer will know that that person may not be a good fit. If the applicant has the sense to make things private which are personal or which may reflect badly on them professionally, then that applicant is probably a good potential employee.

Another reason employers should not be given access to private media is because of the potential for discrimination. Many people use social media to connect with others on a personal level, which may be related to their religion, their gender and sexual orientation, or their political views, all of which could subject an employee to discrimination by an employer. Although an applicant may be better off not being offered a job by a discriminatory employer, we all need jobs and no one should have to risk losing a job because personal proclivities were made public by a snooping potential employer.

Social media should be viewed no differently than one's home and one's mailbox when it comes to privacy. We all have a measure of control over what we make public on the internet, and employers should respect that and judge us personally based only over what we choose for others to see. There are plenty of more relevant qualifiers when determining job applicants than the content of their personal messages. Allowing employers to snoop in this manner would set a dangerous precedent for privacy in our digital lives, which are quickly becoming inseparable from the rest of our lives.

Essay Prompt 2: Medium Scoring Essay (Score of 7 – 9)

Snooping into private social media profiles is absolutely not acceptable by employers or by anybody. Private information is not relevant to the way a person acts professionally. Also, doing this sets a dangerous precedent for privacy rights. Employers should absolutely not be allowed to ask applicants for their social media passwords. If you refuse, then you are less likely to get hired, and that is an unfair burden to put on people trying to find a job.

Students today use Facebook for email and messaging, private applications which have no bearing on public image. An employer asking a teenager for user access to her Facebook profile might just ask well ask for the passwords to her personal email account and her voicemail as well. It is simply an invasion of privacy on a scale that is not acceptable in today's marketplace. No one, potential employers included, is allowed to open someone's mail in their mailbox; why should they be allowed to read Facebook mail?

Employers can still do what anyone else can do – perform a Google search on a person. Through that, they can view all the information about a person which is public. Since that is the information that potential customers of a company can see about the employees, then that should be perfectly sufficient in screening applicants. If an applicant has a Facebook profile which is made public and full of obscenities, slurs, and references to getting wasted, then the employer will know that that person may not be a good fit. If the applicant has the sense to make things private which are personal or which may reflect badly on them professionally, then that applicant is probably a good potential employee.

Social media should be viewed no differently than one's home and one's mailbox when it comes to privacy. There are plenty of more relevant qualifiers when determining job applicants than the content of their personal messages. Allowing employers to snoop in this manner would set a dangerous precedent for privacy in our digital lives, which are quickly becoming inseparable from the rest of our lives.

Essay Prompt 2: Low Scoring Essay (Score of 2 – 6)

Snooping into private social media profiles is absolutely not acceptable by employers or by anybody. Private information is not relevant to the way a person acts professionally. Also, doing this sets a dangerous precedent for privacy rights. Employers should absolutely not be allowed to ask applicants for their social media passwords. If you refuse, then you are less likely to get hired, and that is an unfair burden to put on people trying to find a job. An employer asking a teenager for user access to her Facebook profile might just ask well ask for the passwords to her personal email account and her voicemail as well. It is simply an invasion of privacy on a scale that is not acceptable in today's marketplace. No one, potential employers included, is allowed to open someone's mail in their mailbox; why should they be allowed to read Facebook mail?

Social media should be viewed no differently than one's home and one's mailbox when it comes to privacy. There are plenty of more relevant qualifiers when determining job applicants than the content of their personal messages. Allowing employers to snoop in this manner would set a dangerous precedent for privacy in our digital lives, which are quickly becoming inseparable from the rest of our lives.

Essay Prompt 3

Essay Prompt 3: High Scoring Essay (Score of 10 – 12)

Students who are planning a gap year may envision months-long treks through European cities, interesting and lucrative employment opportunities, and good times unmarred by the rigors of a freshman year of college. However, what they are more likely to find are prohibitive travel costs, minimum wage jobs, and lonely weekends spent at home while their peers are off discovering college life. While a gap year makes sense for some, it is not a good idea for most high school graduates because of these reasons.

Some students plan to work "in the real world" for a year before beginning college. On average, those who earn a Bachelor's degree start their careers earning around $15,000 more than high school graduates. For this reason, it does not make sense to delay the start of college in order to work and earn money. While a lot of skills and life lessons can be learned at the kinds of jobs that do not require a college degree, it is best for a student who plans on going to college to take on those jobs during summers and weekends and not to delay enrolling in college. Imagine a five-year period: a young person can graduate high school and work a minimum-wage job for a year before going to college full time for four years, or start college right away, finish in four years, and then spend a year working at a higher-paying job. Ultimately, the student who chooses the second path will make more money in that same time period.

Many students fantasize of taking a year off before college to travel, imagining that they will explore interesting places across the globe, meet wonderful people, and learn much more than they ever would in a classroom. First of all, the reality is that these types of trips are very expensive and only a few students have families which are able to afford them. Secondly, the opportunities made available to students to travel during college in semester abroad program would ultimately provide a more rewarding experience for most students. Within these programs, students have access to resources like staying with local families rather than in hostels, and taking classes at local universities in a foreign country. By waiting a year or two and then traveling within one of these programs, a student can have a much more meaningful travel experience.

Some students protest that they do not yet know what they want to study and need this time to explore their interests. However, there is no worse way to explore one's academic proclivities than by refusing to go to school. If students want to minimize their educational costs while they figure out what they want to study, they should apply for scholarships and take classes at community colleges. 99 out of 100 students who say that they are taking time off to do some academic soul-searching without taking any classes end up spending that year playing video games and watching television without figuring out a direction. Learning is an overwhelming process, and imposing some structure on it goes a long way.

There is a lot to be said for having unstructured time to explore the world and explore one's own self. However, for the reasons expounded above, it is best not to use a full year after high school graduation as that time. Few students may have genuinely enriching opportunities to fill that time before going to college, but for the vast majority of us, there's no reason to put off the learning opportunities that college has to offer. Not to mention, the year after school, college is where the party will be.

Essay Prompt 3: Medium Scoring Essay (Score of 7 – 9)

Students who are planning a gap year may think of months-long treks through European cities, interesting and lucrative employment opportunities, and good times free from the rigors of a freshman year of college. However, what they are more likely to find are prohibitive travel costs and minimum wage. While a gap year makes sense for some, it is not a good idea for most high school graduates because of these reasons.

Some students plan to work "in the real world" for a year before beginning college. On average, those who earn a Bachelor's degree start their careers earning much more money than high school graduates. For this reason, it does not make sense to delay the start of college in order to work and earn money. While a lot of skills and life lessons can be learned at the kinds of jobs that do not require a college degree, it is best for a student who plans on going to college to take on those jobs during summers and weekends and not to delay enrolling in college. Going to college right away will result in making more money.

Many students fantasize of taking a year off before college to travel, imagining that they will explore interesting places across the globe, meet wonderful people, and learn much more than they ever would in a classroom. The reality is that these types of trips are very expensive and only a few students have families which are able to afford them. Maybe you will be able to study abroad later on in college, but trying to fund a trip on your own in a foreign country is going to be very difficult and expensive, if your parents will even let you go.

There is a lot to be said for having unstructured time to explore the world and explore one's own self. However, for the reasons given above, it is best not to use a full year after high school graduation as that time. Few students may have genuinely enriching opportunities to fill that time before going to college, but for the vast majority of us, there's no reason to put off the learning opportunities that college has to offer. Not to mention, the year after school, college is where the party will be.

Essay Prompt 3: Low Scoring Essay (Score of 2 – 6)

Taking a year off before going to college is a stupid idea. Students might think that they will get to do all kinds of interesting things, but the reality is that most won't be able to afford to do those things. Really, it's just better to go ahead and go to college, where great opportunities are available and it's possible that you'll be able to work a higher-paying job. Some students plan to work "in the real world" for a year before beginning college. On average, those who earn a Bachelor's degree start their careers earning much more money than high school graduates. For this reason, it does not make sense to delay the start of college in order to work and earn money. While a lot of skills and life lessons can be learned at the kinds of jobs that do not require a college degree, it is best for a student who plans on going to college to take on those jobs during summers and weekends and not to delay enrolling in college. Going to college right away will result in making more money.

There is a lot to be said for having unstructured time to explore the world and explore one's own self. However, for the reason given above, it is best not to use a full year after high school graduation as that time.

Chapter 13: Final Thoughts

In the end, we know that you will be successful in taking the ACT. Although getting into the school of your choice can be challenging, if you continue your hard work and dedication (just like you are doing to prepare for the ACT), you will find that your efforts will pay off.

If you are struggling after reading this book and following our guidelines, we sincerely hope that you will take note of our advice and seek additional help. Start by asking friends about the resources that they are using. If you are still not reaching the score you want, consider getting the help of an ACT tutor.

If you are on a budget and cannot afford a private tutoring service, there are plenty of independent tutors, including college students who are proficient in ACT subjects. Remember, the ACT is just a test to get INTO college; it does not test college-level materials. You don't have to spend thousands of dollars to afford a good tutor or review course.

We wish you the best of luck and happy studying. Most importantly, we hope you enjoy your coming college years – after all, you put a lot of work into getting there in the first place.

Sincerely,
The Accepted, Inc. Team

STUDY SMARTER. SCORE HIGHER. GET ACCEPTED.

CPSIA information can be obtained at www.ICGtesting.com
Printed in the USA
LVOW11s1357120114

369091LV00021B/755/P

9 780989 818858